THE DEVIL IN THE HOLY CITY

HOW THE CATHOLIC CHURCH CORRUPTED CHRISTIANITY

THE EXPOSÉ BABYLON TRILOGY
BOOK 1

BRIAN MALEK

REVELATIONS
MEDIA

Fair Use & Copyright Notice

Revised Legal & Fair Use Notice

This book is a work of investigative nonfiction.

It examines historical records, theological doctrines, publicly available documents, and Scripture for the purposes of criticism, commentary, education, and scholarship.

Scripture Permissions

Media, Rights & Licensing

For permissions, interviews, or licensing inquiries, contact:

info@brianmalek.com

DEDICATION

To Jesus — my Deliverer, my Shepherd, and the source of all truth. Whose love is unrelenting, whose grace is undeserved, and whose patience with me defies reason. I haven't always made it easy, but I am forever grateful.

To my wife — my compass, my flame, and the one for whom I'd burn Babylon to the ground. Without her, this book would not exist. I likely would have remained within the Roman Catholic system, never finding the courage to seek the truth. Her guidance, patience, and those ever-so-subtle nudges toward His Word led me out of darkness. I would still be lost without her.

To Ed Kurath — my friend and mentor, a world-renowned author and Christian counselor whose teachings on transformation and sanctification helped Brandy and me draw closer to Jesus. His wisdom, counsel, and discernment played an instrumental role in shaping this book. We've had many long conversations about the actual teachings of

Christ — and how religion has distorted or buried them. Without Ed, this book might have contained more darkness than light.

And to Ace and Bailey *— my two Jack Russell Terriers. Never more than a few feet away while I wrote. Your quiet presence was the anchor I didn't know I needed.*

Ace & Bailey: My Jack Russell Terriers

CONTENTS

AUTHOR'S NOTE
WHY I HAD TO WRITE THIS BOOK

What if one of the world's oldest and most influential religious institutions—an organization that has shaped Western civilization, politics, and theology—was never what it claimed to be?

What if the towering cathedrals, ancient rituals, and solemn traditions that millions associate with holiness are not signs of divine authority, but the outer shell of something far older, more complex, and far more dangerous?

This book is not a denominational critique, nor a work of casual theological disagreement. It is a historical, biblical, and spiritual investigation into a claim so deeply ingrained that few dare to question it: that the Roman Catholic Church represents the Body of Christ on earth.

I did not set out to write this book lightly.

I was raised in the Roman Catholic system. I honored it, trusted it, and submitted to its authority. Many of my friends and family remain practicing Catholics, and this work was never intended as an attack on individual believers. My concern is not with sincere faith, but with institutional power—specifically, with a religious system that claims divine authority while redefining the gospel itself.

As my research deepened, what began as discomfort turned into a pattern—one that could not be ignored. The deeper I traced the Church's origins, doctrines, and historical alliances, the clearer it became that something fundamental was wrong. Not merely flawed. Not merely corrupted over time. But structurally misaligned from the very message Jesus and the apostles proclaimed.

This book documents that journey.

Growing up in the Catholic Church, I always felt as if something wasn't right, but I couldn't put my finger on it. The deeper I went—through prayer, study, and uncomfortable honesty—the clearer the divide became between what Jesus taught and what the Church practiced. Between the simplicity of the gospel and the weight of institutional authority. What I had been raised in increasingly resembled Rome more than Christ.

Then, one day, everything changed.

After surviving a mountain biking accident that should have left me paralyzed—or worse—I was forced to confront a question I could no longer avoid: *What if the Church isn't what it claims to be?*

Jesus warned,

> "Watch out for false prophets. They come to you in sheep's clothing, but inwardly they are ravenous wolves." (Matthew 7:15)

The Catholic Church claims to represent Christ. But does it reflect His Spirit?

Catholic doctrine differs in critical ways from the teaching of Scripture. The Vatican teaches that Peter was the first pope, that Mary functions as a co-mediator, and that salvation is administered through sacramental authority. Scripture teaches something far simpler—and far more direct:

> *"There is one mediator between God and man—the man Christ Jesus." (1 Timothy 2:5)*

> *"All have sinned and fall short of the glory of God." (Romans 3:23)*

> *"It is by grace you have been saved, through faith—not by works." (Ephesians 2:8–9)*

These are not secondary disagreements. They are foundational.

The New Testament teaches that the true Church is not a hierarchy of offices or a succession of titles, but a living body transformed from within by the indwelling Spirit of God. Yet over centuries, that message was displaced by a system that emphasized conformity over transformation, obedience over regeneration, and authority over truth.

Scripture warned this would happen.

> *"From among your own selves will arise men speaking twisted things, to draw away the disciples after them." (Acts 20:30)*

> *"There will be false teachers among you... and many will follow their destructive ways." (2 Peter 2:1–2)*

The greatest deception is not atheism. It is religion that appears holy, quotes Scripture, and invokes Christ—while serving another authority entirely.

"Satan disguises himself as an angel of light... so it is no surprise if his servants also disguise themselves as servants of righteousness." (2 Corinthians 11:13–15)

This deception did not stop at Rome. Its influence spread—into Protestant denominations, seminaries, and modern Christianity itself. The result is a global religious culture that often bears the name of Christ while lacking the power of the gospel He preached.

This book is written for those who have felt that tension—for readers who sense that something is wrong but cannot quite articulate why. It is for those weary of lifeless religion and hungry for authentic spiritual renewal. And it is for those willing to examine uncomfortable truths in pursuit of genuine faith.

The Devil in the Holy City serves as the foundation for a larger investigation. It exposes the origins of a counterfeit religious system and establishes the framework for understanding what followed. The books that follow will examine how that system adapted, expanded, and positioned itself for a modern world shaped by technology, globalization, and unprecedented forms of control.

But this volume stands on its own.

If the claims in these chapters disturb you, take your time. Test them. Measure them against Scripture. Examine the sources. Truth does not fear scrutiny.

My purpose is not to tear down what is holy, but to expose what is counterfeit—so that what is true may finally be seen clearly.

Jesus warned of wolves in sheep's clothing. The book of Revelation warned of a religious power that appears righteous while opposing the Spirit of God. This book asks whether those warnings were symbolic abstractions—or historical realities.

We are living in serious times. The stakes are not denominational loyalty or religious identity, but spiritual freedom itself.

If you continue, do so prayerfully. Let the evidence speak. Let Scripture remain your authority. And above all, seek the living Christ—not an institution that claims to represent Him.

"Come out of her, My people, so that you will not share in her sins." (Revelation 18:4)

~

Take a breath. Say a prayer. And turn the page.

A READER'S CAUTION BEFORE DISMISSAL
BEFORE YOU REJECT THIS BOOK

You may think this is just another anti-Catholic propaganda book. I understand why.

Before you decide this is "just another attack on the Catholic Church," pause for a moment. This section is not an argument. It's a caution label—read it before you walk away.

What would it take for you to seriously consider that something you've believed your entire life might be wrong?

Because if you had handed me this book years ago, I would have been skeptical, too, because I was raised Catholic.

At first, I loved the pageantry, the discipline, the sacred rhythms of the liturgical year. I believed—sincerely—that it was the one true Church of Jesus Christ.

That belief didn't collapse overnight. It cracked slowly, under questions that never received clear answers. Not from the Catechism. Not from priests. Not from Rome.

Questions like:

- Why does the Church teach that salvation is mediated through sacraments when Scripture says it is by grace through faith?
- Why does the Bible declare Jesus the sole mediator between God and man, while the Church assigns that role to Mary and the priesthood?
- Why does the New Testament describe a spiritual priesthood of all believers, yet Rome insists on a hierarchical caste of clergy?
- Why does the Church elevate tradition to the level of Scripture when Jesus explicitly warned against doing so?

I know what you might be thinking. *"This is just another anti-Catholic rant."*

It isn't.

This book is not written to mock, insult, or attack believers. It is a plea to test what you've been taught—to examine whether the system you trust actually aligns with the words and warnings of Jesus and the apostles.

If Catholicism is correct, then this book will not survive scrutiny. Close it. Discard it. Move on.

But if it's wrong—even partially wrong—if it has added to the gospel, redefined salvation, or placed religious authority between you and Christ, wouldn't you want to know?

Wouldn't truth be worth the discomfort?

You don't have to agree with me. You don't have to like me. But before you dismiss what follows, ask yourself one honest question:

What if he's right?

Because once evidence is examined, it cannot be unseen. And once the gospel is encountered apart from institutional mediation, it becomes difficult to confuse faith with system again.

"Test all things; hold fast what is good." (1 Thessalonians 5:21)

THE MOST DANGEROUS DECEPTION IS THE ONE THAT APPEARS HOLY

*"Watch out for false prophets, who come to you in
sheep's clothing but inwardly are voracious wolves."
(Matthew 7:15).*

For nearly two thousand years, a spiritual system has operated at the heart of Christianity—claiming to represent Jesus Christ, while quietly rewriting His message, burying His promises, and enthroning man in place of God.

This is not an accusation against individual believers, but against an institutional system.

This book isn't just about history.

It's about deception.

What if the world's largest religious institution isn't the Bride of Christ—but the woman who rides the beast (Revelation 17:1–7)?

What if the most respected Christian empire is actually the greatest counterfeit in religious history?

Jesus warned that "false christs and false prophets will appear and perform great signs and wonders to deceive, if possible, even the elect" (Matthew 24:24).

Paul echoed it—that a great delusion would come upon those who refused to love the truth (2 Thessalonians 2:10–11).

What if that delusion is already here—and it wears a cross?

I was born into this system.

I served it.

I defended it.

I trusted it.

But then something changed.

I encountered Jesus—not the Jesus of rituals and rules, but the Jesus of Scripture.

I should have been paralyzed or died that day on the mountain. I didn't. And what I realized in that hospital bed changed everything.

The Jesus who saves by grace, speaks through His Spirit, and tears down the walls between man and God.

Once I saw the truth, I couldn't go back.

This book is my testimony—and a warning. It dismantles centuries-old claims passed down through tradition, councils, catechisms, and pulpits. It is a line-by-line unmasking of how the Roman Church absorbed paganism, corrupted the gospel, and built a global religious empire in Christ's name—but not through His Spirit.

Many inside it are sincere. But the system they serve is not.

More than that, this book is a call to freedom.

If you've ever questioned what you were taught...

If you've ever felt something was off but couldn't explain it...

If you love Jesus but feel distant from the structure that claims to represent Him...

This book is for you.

It's not anti-Catholic.

It's pro-truth.

It's not an attack.

It's an invitation—to come out, to wake up, to be transformed.

You don't need a priest.

You don't need a pope.

You don't need permission.

You need Jesus.

And the time to find Him—truly, fully, and without tradition standing in the way—is now.

> *"Come out of her, My people, so that you will not share in her sins." (Revelation 18:4).*

READER ORIENTATION:
A MENTAL CHECKPOINT

Before we go any further, there's something you need to understand—because even truth can bounce off a programmed mind.

You've been conditioned to think in certain patterns.

Words trigger responses before reason has time to engage.

Say *paramedic*, and most people think: safety, rescue, trust.

Say *parachute*, and they think: protection, controlled descent, survival.

Now say *paranormal*.

For many, the reaction is immediate: irrational, fringe, dismissed.

But that response isn't the product of careful thought. It's conditioning.

The reality is simple: many phenomena labeled "paranormal" are simply things not yet understood within prevailing frameworks.

Fifty years ago, a smartphone would have been considered

magic, sorcery, or witchcraft. Today, it sits in your pocket. The category didn't change—the understanding did.

Human history is filled with examples of things we were certain about... until we were wrong.

On this subject, we have likely been wrong for a very long time.

Jesus understood this dynamic clearly. He repeatedly confronted not ignorance, but *mental frameworks*—systems of belief so deeply ingrained that truth could pass directly through them without being received.

That is why He spoke of eyes that do not see and ears that do not hear.

As you read this book, you will encounter ideas that challenge assumptions you may not even realize you hold. Some concepts may trigger immediate resistance—not because they are false, but because they fall outside the boundaries you were trained to accept.

This is not an invitation to abandon discernment. It is an invitation to suspend reflexive dismissal.

The real question is not whether something feels unfamiliar or uncomfortable.

The real question is this:

What else have we been taught to reject without ever examining the evidence?

Keep that question in mind as you begin.

With that mental framework in place, one more distinction must be made before we proceed.

BEFORE YOU CONFUSE
CHURCH WITH CHRIST

Before you read another page, I need you to separate two things most people treat as identical:

Jesus Christ and "church."

If those two words collapse into one category in your mind—if "church" automatically means "God's people," "God's will," or "God's approval"—then even truth can slide right past you. You will mistake structure for salvation. Attendance for obedience. Tradition for transformation. And you will feel spiritually safe while remaining spiritually unchanged.

The gospel does not call people to behave better—it calls them to **become new**, transformed from within by the indwelling Spirit of God, not managed from without by religious systems.

This is not a warning aimed at sincere believers. It is aimed at a mental habit—a reflex—trained into people over the course of decades: the assumption that proximity to religious activity equals proximity to Christ.

It does not.

The Pharisees had proximity. They had Scripture. They had

tithes, fasts, prayers, and weekly services. They had reputation. They had position. And Jesus still told them the unthinkable: their hearts were not aligned with God. They loved the appearance of holiness more than its reality. They clung to structure while resisting the Spirit.

This should terrify every religious person alive.

Because an hour in a building can become a substitute for surrender. A weekly routine can become a counterfeit assurance. And a church culture can inoculate you against the actual gospel —by giving you enough religion to feel righteous without ever becoming new.

God is not impressed by the costume.

God is not moved by the schedule.

God is not fooled by ritual.

He demands truth in the inward parts—repentance, obedience, and living faith.

The New Testament does not present Christianity as a once-a-week event. It presents it as a life—Christ reigning in the whole person. Not public performance, but private holiness. Not external conformity, but internal transformation.

That is why Jesus didn't establish a priestly-state hierarchy to mediate salvation.

He didn't recruit people into a religious machine.

He called them to follow Him.

His earliest followers weren't known as "The Cathedral People."

They were called the Way.

Not a brand or a denomination but a direction — a path.

Jesus preached in fields, streets, and homes. He challenged religious power more than He courted it. He did not teach men to place God inside buildings and then manage Him through offices, titles, and intermediaries. He preached a kingdom that pierces the heart—one that confronts the conscience and demands the whole person.

And yes—this is where some will object:

"But didn't Jesus establish the Church?"

He established His people.
He established His Body.
He established a living community, built on Himself, animated by His Spirit, and governed by truth.

What He did not establish was a Roman-style hierarchy of control that claims exclusive authority over salvation.

The New Testament model is radically simple:

- Christ is the Head
- The Spirit is the indwelling power
- Believers are the living stones

Any system that replaces that with ritual, offices, and institutional gatekeeping is not a harmless variation. It is a change in kind. A shift from relationship to management. From direct access to mediated access. From transformation to control.

For the first centuries after Jesus, believers gathered in homes, caves, and small communities—often under threat, often persecuted, often without political power. They had no cathedrals, no imperial budgets, no global headquarters, and no state enforcement. They followed Christ, knowing it could cost them their reputation, safety, livelihood, or even their lives—without cathedrals, political protection, or institutional cover.

Then history turned.

In A.D. 313, Christianity was legalized under Emperor Constantine. Shortly after, church leadership began merging with the empire. And when the Roman state adopted Christian language, Christianity did not simply "win." It was reorganized—and inevitably politicized.

This is not conspiracy talk. It is a historical fact: institutions, by their nature, seek control. When spiritual truth becomes a tool of political unity, the message gets managed. The edges get sanded down. The kingdom becomes a system. The faith becomes an institution. And the institution becomes powerful.

That is the shift you must keep in mind as you read this book.

Because the deception is not merely that Rome became influential. The deception is that Rome presented its religious structure as the Body of Christ, and millions accepted the claim without testing it.

So ask yourself, honestly:

- Have you been trained to believe that your standing with God is measured by attendance?
- Have you been taught to treat a building as "God's house," as if the living God can be confined to stone?
- Have you replaced obedience with participation?
- Have you confused spiritual life with religious activity?

If so, you are not alone.

But you are in danger of mistaking religion for regeneration. Not because church gatherings are inherently evil—Scripture shows believers gathering. The danger is when the gathering becomes the substitute.

When the system becomes the mediator.

When tradition becomes the authority.

When "church" becomes the thing you trust instead of Christ.

Here is the dividing line you must hold onto:

- The gospel is not "show up."
- The gospel is "die to self and live in Christ."
- Not one hour of religious routine.
- A full surrender of your life.
- Not a badge.
- A rebirth.
- Not external performance.
- Internal regeneration.

And that is why this book matters.

Because if you confuse church with Christ, you can be deeply religious and still lost. You can be surrounded by sermons and still remain unchanged. You can know the vocabulary of faith and still be far from the living God.

Jesus warned about wolves in sheep's clothing for a reason.

Paul warned about another gospel for a reason.

The book of Revelation warns about a system that appears holy while intoxication spreads through the nations for a reason.

This is not about winning arguments. It is about seeing clearly.

So before you proceed, lock this into your mind:

- Attendance is not obedience.
- Ritual is not righteousness.
- Institution is not salvation.
- And "church" is not Christ.

Now you're ready.

Proceed—slowly, prayerfully, and with the courage to test everything against Scripture.

CHAPTER 0 — KNOW YOUR ENEMY
THE LUCIFERIAN ROOT
BENEATH THE VATICAN

Before we proceed, we need to clarify one more thing: this is not just a book about corruption. It's a spiritual war briefing—one grounded in Scripture, discernment, and truth, not violence or hostility toward people. The enemy is older and more cunning than any religious system—including the popes and priests who serve within it.

The First Rule of War

Every general knows: you can't win a war if you don't know who you're fighting. You must study your enemy—his methods, disguises, strongholds, and tactics. You must map the battlefield. You must understand the psychology of deception.

But most Christians walk into the spiritual warzone of modern life unaware that a war is even taking place. They might see corruption, abuse, or manipulation in the Church—but they don't trace it back to the source.

They think the problem is political.

They think it's institutional.
They think it's human.
But the Word of God says otherwise:

> "For we wrestle not against flesh and blood, but against
> principalities, against powers, against the rulers of
> the darkness of this world, against spiritual wicked-
> ness in high places." (Ephesians 6:12, KJV)

This book will uncover lies, expose agendas, and document historical responsibility—but don't be fooled. The real enemy isn't a cardinal in Rome or a bishop in Chicago. It's the ancient serpent who has worked for millennia to infiltrate, hijack, and imitate the things of God.

You're not holding a theology textbook. You're holding a guide to **spiritual resistance**—resisting deception through discernment, Scripture, and truth.

Lucifer's Strategy: Deception Through Devotion

Satan doesn't always wear horns. Sometimes he wears robes. He doesn't always show up with hate. Sometimes he shows up with holiness. Paul warned the Church long ago:

> "For Satan himself is transformed into an angel of light.
> Therefore it is no great thing if his ministers also be
> transformed as the ministers of righteousness." (2
> Corinthians 11:14–15)

Lucifer doesn't need to turn people into rebels.
He just needs to keep them religious.
He needs ritual to replace righteousness.

Tradition to replace truth.

Systems to replace salvation.

He's not trying to make atheists.

He's trying to make worshipers of a counterfeit Christ.

The Battle Map

In the pages ahead, you'll see how this spiritual enemy has:

- Infiltrated the Church through centuries of doctrinal distortion
- Weaponized ritual, relics, and reverence against the very people they claim to sanctify
- Built a counterfeit kingdom that spans the globe while masquerading as the bride of Christ

The evidence is not just historical. It's current.

The deception is not just theological. It's spiritual.

And the system is not merely broken—it was engineered.

We will identify historical actors, doctrines, and systems.

We will trace ideas.

We will test every tradition against the Word of God.

But if you forget everything else, remember this:

"Know your enemy and know yourself, and you will not be defeated in a hundred battles." —Sun Tzu, *The Art of War*

The Church today is being defeated because it no longer knows either. Even satire has noticed. As *The Babylon Bee* recently joked:

"Christians Decide To Put Aside Their Petty Differences And Unite For The Gospel—Haha Just Kidding, We're Fighting Each Other Online."[1]

It's funny because it's true. While deception strategizes, believers argue over clickbait theology and performative outrage. And that is precisely what the enemy wants: confusion, division, and religious infighting disguised as righteousness.

The serpent's greatest disguise is not atheism.

It is organized religion without the Spirit.

You cannot defeat what you refuse to see.

And Satan's greatest victory was convincing the Church that he retired.

This book is not an attack.

It is a countermeasure—an act of exposure, not aggression.

Notes

1. "Christians Decide to Put Aside Their Petty Differences and Unite for the Gospel—Haha Just Kidding, We're Fighting Each Other Online," *The Babylon Bee*, June 14, 2024, https://babylonbee.com/news/christians-decide-to-put-aside-their-petty-differences-and-unite-for-the-gospel-haha-just-kidding-were-fighting-each-other-online.

PART I

THE SETUP

HOW DECEPTION TOOK HOLD

1

THE PERFECT COVER

HOW ROME USED RELIGION
TO HIDE AN EMPIRE

*"My people are destroyed for lack of knowledge." (Hosea
4:6).*

*As Edward Kurath notes, this is not a declaration of annihilation but of
spiritual consequence — God's heartbreak over willful ignorance.*[1]

It's remarkable how life can change in an instant.

I was on a mountain biking trip in Steamboat Springs,
Colorado—an adventure I'd been looking forward to. The
sun was shining, the trail was perfect, and I felt alive, invincible
even. But in an instant, everything shifted.

I lost control. I crashed hard. I slammed head-first into the
rocky ground, and I knew immediately something was very
wrong. I heard the crunching of my neck—but strangely, felt no
pain.

In that desperate moment, I did the only thing I could. I cried
out, "Jesus, help me!"

Somehow, despite the severity of my injury, I was able to get up and walk out of the woods with a broken neck—I completely shattered my C4 and C5 vertebrae. The doctors were amazed I wasn't paralyzed, or worse. By all human logic, I should've been.

But I wasn't. I was alive. And I knew why.

It wasn't because of luck. It wasn't because of the doctors' skill. It was because Jesus heard my cry.

This wasn't the first time He'd saved my life. Looking back, I realize there were multiple instances—close calls that I'd shrugged off as coincidence or good fortune. But now, it was undeniable: God had been preserving me, pursuing me, even when I didn't fully acknowledge Him.

Shortly after my accident, my wife shared something with me that shook me even further. She told me that while she was praying for me, she had a vision. She saw Jesus standing over me on the mountain, holding my broken neck in His hands, keeping me from being paralyzed or killed.

When she described it, she wasn't emotional or trying to be dramatic. She simply stated it as fact—the way someone would describe the sunrise or the sound of rain. It felt as real to her as the ground beneath her feet.

To spare her the pain, I hadn't shared any details of my crash with her.

That was the moment I realized this wasn't just about surviving an accident—this was a wake-up call. God wasn't just saving my life. He was calling me out—calling me out of the dead, ritualistic religion I'd trusted for so long and into a real, living relationship with Him.

I was raised Catholic. I went to Catholic schools. I memorized the prayers, attended the sacraments, and obeyed the Church's teachings. I thought I knew God because I was familiar with the Catholic religion.

But in that hospital bed, reflecting on what had just happened, I realized I'd never truly known Him.

The Roman Catholic system taught me about rules, rituals, and hierarchy. It taught me to trust the Church more than Christ. It offered me sacraments instead of salvation and tradition instead of transformation.

It wasn't enough. It was never enough. I needed something more —something real. I needed Jesus, not religion.

The truth is, I'd carried doubts about the Catholic Church and her man-made dogmas for most of my adult life. There were teachings that never fully sat right with me, practices that seemed to

contradict Scripture. But I could never quite put my finger on it—or prove it—until now.

The accident—and everything that followed—forced me to confront what I'd long suspected: there was something fundamentally wrong at the core of the Roman Catholic system.

This realization set me on a path I never expected to walk.

As I recovered physically, I began to seek God with new eyes. I opened the Bible for myself, no longer filtered through the lens of Catholic dogma. I started researching Church history—not the sanitized version presented in Catholic schools, but the raw, unfiltered truth.

What I found horrified me. The Roman Catholic Church wasn't just slightly off course. It was a complete distortion of the gospel.

Layer by layer, the facade crumbled: pagan traditions baptized into Christian practice. Political corruption fused with religious power. Doctrines and dogmas that contradicted Scripture. A system built on fear, control, and deception. It wasn't the Church that Jesus Christ founded. It was a counterfeit kingdom built in His name.

I didn't want to believe it at first. I wrestled with it. I tried to find ways to reconcile what I'd been taught with what I was now learning. But the more I prayed, the more I studied, the clearer it became: I'd been deceived.

If you're Catholic, there's a good chance you've had a similar conversation with one of your friends or loved ones...

A Talk Between Friends

Joe: I'm Catholic. Born and raised, baptized, confirmed, and loyal to the Church. I'm not looking to leave it.

Luke: I get it. I was in the same place. I'm not trying to pull you out of anything. I want to ask something.

Joe: Go ahead.

Luke: If the Catholic Church taught something that directly contradicted the Bible... which one would you follow?

Joe: I don't believe it contradicts the Bible. That's Protestant spin.

Luke: I used to think that, too. But what if I could show you? Not with opinion — with Scripture. Would you want to see it?

Joe: Maybe. But I already know the Church gave us the Bible. And she's the one who can interpret it correctly.

Luke: But that's the question. What if she's not interpreting it... what if she's overriding it?

Joe: Like what?

Luke: Like the Mass. The Bible says Jesus was sacrificed once for all. But the Church says the Mass is a "re-presentation" of the same sacrifice. That's not just semantics. That's an entirely different gospel.

Joe: You're misunderstanding Catholic teaching.

Luke: I thought so, too. But the more I dug, the more I saw it clearly. We're told the bread becomes Christ's literal flesh. Yet Jesus said, "The Spirit gives life; the flesh counts for nothing." And Paul warned against crucifying Christ again and again.

Joe: But that's what the Church has always taught.

Luke: That's what Rome taught. But the early Christians didn't teach that. They saw communion as a remembrance, not a mystical flesh ritual. They didn't worship a wafer. They worshipped Christ by Spirit and truth.

Joe: So you think millions of Catholics are wrong?

Luke: I think millions of Catholics are sincere. But sincerity can't save us. Only Jesus can. And He said, "The truth will set you free."

Study Box: What Did Jesus Really Mean by "Eat My Flesh"?

In John 6, Jesus begins by using the Greek word *phagō* (φαγώ) — meaning "to eat" in the ordinary sense. Later, He switches to *trōgō* (τρώγω), a more graphic word meaning "to gnaw or chew."[2] Catholic apologists claim this proves literal consumption. But Jesus wasn't speaking biologically — He was using hyperbole to shock the crowd and expose their carnal mindset.

THE CLINCHER?

. . .

HE FINISHES BY SAYING: "The Spirit gives life; the flesh profits nothing" (John 6:63).

If He meant literal flesh, He would've contradicted His entire point.

"I'm not attacking your faith. I'm exposing the system that hijacked it." — from A Talk Between Friends.

That conversation stuck with me because Joe's questions were once mine, too.

And if I, someone who genuinely loved God, could be so thoroughly deceived, how many others were still trapped? How many souls were still shackled to a system that could never save them?

This book is the result of that journey. It's not written out of anger or bitterness. It's written out of love—for the truth, for the Body of Christ, and for every soul still ensnared by the Roman system.

I'm not here to tear down what's holy. I'm here to expose what's counterfeit. I know the cost. I know the backlash. But I can't stay silent.

If you're willing to take an honest look—if you're willing to set aside tradition and test everything against the Word of God—I believe you'll see the same truth that set me free.

You'll see that the Roman Catholic Church isn't the Body of Christ. It's the woman who rides the beast. But you'll also see something even greater: that Jesus Christ is still calling His people out of Babylon. That transformation is still possible. That true freedom is found not in a system, but in Him.

"Come out of her, My people, so that you will not share in her sins." (Revelation 18:4).

As Edward Kurath notes, this is not a threat of annihilation but a call to decisive spiritual separation — a declaration of consequence, not destruction.[3]

Notes

1. Edward Kurath, *Transformation Epistles*, rev. ed. (Post Falls, ID: Divinely Designed, 2019), 28.

2. James Strong, *The Exhaustive Concordance of the Bible* (Nashville: Abingdon, 1890), entries G5315 and G5176.

3. Kurath, *Transformation Epistles*, 232.

THE BLUEPRINT OF CONTROL

FROM CONSTANTINE TO THE VATICAN — ENGINEERING SPIRITUAL SUBMISSION

"For there are many rebellious people, full of meaning-less talk and deception, especially those of the circumcision group. They must be silenced, because they are disrupting whole households by teaching things they ought not to teach." (Titus 1:10–11).

It wasn't until I looked back at my own journey that I realized how deeply deceived I'd been.

For most of my life, I thought I was saved—not because of anything I'd done, but because I'd embraced a system that claimed to represent Jesus Christ. I thought the Catholic Church had the answers, the right way, the truth. The rituals, the rules, the traditions —they were all supposed to point to God, right?

But deep down, I knew something was wrong.

I had doubts. I had questions. I had a gnawing feeling that something didn't align. I started asking questions—quietly at first, trying to reason it out on my own. But each time I dug deeper into the Church's teachings, I found that the structure wasn't setting people free. It was enslaving them. It was distorting the message of Jesus Christ, twisting it, and burying the true gospel beneath layers of tradition and ritual.

The more I learned, the more I realized this wasn't a new deception. This was an age-old lie passed down through generations of religious corruption. A system that disguised itself as the Bride of Christ yet was nothing more than the woman who rides the beast—the Roman Catholic Church, the most powerful and most subtle counterfeit in all of history.

I began to understand the depth of the deception.

THE CHURCH's Corruption Exposed

Vision of the Cross: fresco by Raphael's workshop, Vatican Museums (c. 1520– 1524). Public domain. See Appendix R for citation.

Let's take a moment to step back. I've spent years uncovering the history of the Church. It's not pretty, and it's not easy to digest. But the truth is undeniable.

The Roman Catholic Church, from the very beginning, absorbed pagan traditions, twisted biblical teachings, and consolidated power. What was once pure and holy became contaminated by man-made dogmas. The Pope's seat, once a place of spiritual leadership, became a throne of political control. Layer by layer, the facade crumbled: pagan traditions baptized into Christian practice. Political corruption fused with religious power.

St. Peter's dome: Layer by layer, the façade crumbled—St. Peter's dome (top) was modeled after the Pantheon (bottom), Rome's pagan temple to all gods. The Vatican borrowed not only imperial theology but imperial architecture. See Appendix R for citation.

The Sacraments

THE SACRAMENTAL SYSTEM is built upon traditions that have no basis in Scripture. The Catholic Church created sacraments to control people, making salvation something to be earned by good works and rituals instead of a gift from God through faith alone (Ephesians 2:8–9).

The Seven Sacraments: The Catholic Church teaches that grace is dispensed through seven sacraments—each controlled by clerical authority. Scripture offers no such requirement for salvation by faith. See Appendix R for citation.

The Seven Sacraments of the Roman Catholic Church

THE CATHOLIC CHURCH teaches that God's grace is dispensed through seven formal sacraments—each requiring specific words, actions, and clerical authority. These are:

- **Baptism** – Water poured with the Trinitarian formula by a priest or deacon, believed to remove original sin.
  Confirmation – Anointing with oil by a bishop, sealing the recipient with the Holy Spirit.
- **Eucharist (Communion)** – Bread and wine consecrated by a priest, said to become the literal body and blood of Christ.
- **Penance (Confession)** – Confession of sins to a priest, who declares absolution in God's name.

- **Anointing of the Sick** – Holy oil applied by a priest
  during illness or near death for healing or forgiveness.
- **Holy Orders** – Laying on of hands and words of
  ordination by a bishop, conferring clerical authority.
- **Matrimony** – A sacramental covenant formed by
  mutual consent and exchange of vows, witnessed by
  clergy.

Each sacrament is administered by the institutional hierarchy
and is often required for salvation. Scripture, however, teaches
that salvation is by grace through faith—not through rituals or
priestly mediation.

The Mass

The Roman Mass is centered on the sacrifice of the altar—a
practice that mimics the Jewish sacrifices in the Old Testament.
Yet, the book of Hebrews makes it clear that Jesus Christ's sacrifice
was once and for all and that no other sacrifice is needed
(Hebrews 10:10–14).

The Inquisition

The history of the Catholic Church includes centuries of violence
and intolerance. The Inquisition, an institution of terror, was used
to suppress any belief that contradicted Church doctrine. Millions
were tortured and killed for daring to challenge the official teachings of the Church.

This isn't the Church that Christ founded. It's a counterfeit, a distortion of the true faith.

The Inquisition: One of the darkest chapters in Church history — used torture, fear, and public trials to suppress dissent. Millions suffered in the name of enforced orthodoxy. See Appendix R for citation.

The Church's Roots in Paganism

THE MOST SHOCKING discovery for me was how the Catholic Church adopted pagan practices into its teachings. When the Roman Empire converted to Christianity in the fourth century, pagan practices didn't disappear. Instead, they were baptized into the Church.

- The pagan sun god became Jesus in the Eucharist, with the sun's rays shining down on the wafer.

Coin from the reign of Constantine I honoring Sol Invictus:
Despite his public conversion to Christianity, Constantine
continued minting coins that depicted pagan deities—evidence of
Rome's fusion between imperial cult worship and emerging
Christian symbolism. See Appendix R for citation.

The Virgin Mary was venerated as the new Isis, the mother goddess worshiped by pagans for centuries.

- The pagan holidays of Saturnalia and other celebrations were converted into Christian feasts, such as Christmas and Easter.

The Church created a system where tradition and ritual took precedence over the Word of God. And, even worse, these pagan practices were sold to the people as if they were divinely inspired. The power structure was built to control people, to make them dependent on the Church, and to separate them from the true gospel of salvation by grace alone.

This wasn't accidental. It was systematic. A slow erosion of the truth, which had been taking place for centuries. But it wasn't until I woke up that I saw just how deep the deception ran.

THE WAKE-UP-CALL

IT TOOK me years to finally see the truth for what it was. The Church wasn't just a bit off course. It was corrupted entirely by man-made traditions and political power. It was the opposite of what Jesus came to establish.

But there's good news: Jesus Christ's gospel remains true, and He continues to call people out of this deception. And that's what this book is about:

- Exposing the deception that has enslaved so many in a false gospel.
- Showing how the true gospel of Jesus Christ can set us free.
- Calling you to wake up and see the truth for yourself.

THE REAL CHURCH: Freedom in Christ

- You don't need a priest.
- You don't need a pope.
- You don't need permission from anyone.
- You need Jesus Christ and His free gift of grace.

THE CHURCH ISN'T the building, the rituals, or the hierarchy—it's the Body of Christ, made up of believers who've been set free from the law and death through the finished work of Christ on the cross.

3

WHAT'S THE SOLUTION?

ESCAPING RELIGION — AND REDISCOVERING THE POWER THAT TRANSFORMS

"You will know the truth, and the truth will set you free." (John 8:32).

It's easy to become overwhelmed by the darkness once you begin to see it.

When I first started peeling back the layers of religious tradition and historical corruption, I felt like I'd been punched in the gut. The weight of deception was staggering. How could something claiming to be the one true Church be so saturated with falsehood?

But what stunned me most wasn't just the existence of the deception—it was realizing that the corruption wasn't accidental. It was intentional. It was engineered.

The Roman Catholic Church hadn't fallen into error by mistake. It had been hijacked by design centuries before through a fusion of political ambition, pagan tradition, and spiritual counterfeiting.[1]

. . .

RELIGIOUS SYSTEMS ARE **Predictable**

IF HISTORY TEACHES US ANYTHING, it's that religious systems, once entangled with power, inevitably drift toward control, corruption, and spiritual death. The pattern is painfully familiar:

- Men build institutions in God's name.
- Institutions harden into traditions.
- Truth is replaced with ritual. The Spirit is quenched.
- The people are enslaved.[2]

It happened in ancient Israel. It happened under Rome. It happened throughout the Middle Ages. And it's still happening today.

THE PROTESTANT PROBLEM

THIS ISN'T JUST a Catholic issue. The fingerprints of Rome have also stained Protestantism. What was supposed to be the great corrective —the Reformation—eventually calcified into its own institutions, hierarchies, and doctrinal idols.

Bureaucracy replaced boldness. Denominational loyalty replaced biblical fidelity. Seminaries recycled the same dead Greek logicsystems that Rome used to sterilize the gospel.[3] The result?

Millions of believers today are still caught in a sanitized version of Rome—unaware that their spiritual inheritance has been watered down, misdirected, or buried under theological rubble.

. . .

So . . . What's the Solution?

THE SOLUTION ISN'T:

- Finding the "right" denomination
- Reforming an old system
- Polishing doctrine or perfecting ritual
- Submitting to a new pastor, pope, or prophet

The solution is Jesus Christ Himself. Not the institutionalized Jesus of councils and creeds. Not the intellectual mascot of modern apologetics. Not the sanitized figurehead of powerless religion.

But the living, risen Jesus—who still speaks, still heals, and still transforms hearts.

THE GOSPEL WAS NEVER About Systems

JESUS DIDN'T COME to build a bureaucracy. He came to:

- Set captives free
- Heal the broken
- Destroy the works of the Devil
- Make living temples out of dead men and women

The early Church wasn't a pyramid of bishops and theologians. It was a Spirit-filled movement of ordinary people—bold, free, and unshackled from dead religion. As D. W. Bercot demonstrates in his study of early Christianity, the pre-Constantinian believers emphasized obedience, holiness, and separation from worldly power rather than institutional dominance.[4]

> *"Where the Spirit of the Lord is, there is freedom"* (2 Corinthians 3:17).

WHAT'S BEEN LOST

WHAT WE'VE LOST ISN'T JUST doctrinal purity. We've lost transformation.

Today's churches are overflowing with activity but empty of power. Sermons are polished, but hearts remain unchanged. People confess Christ with their mouths but stay enslaved to the very chains He came to break. That's not salvation. That's spiritual theater.

Ed Kurath, a biblical commentator and translator known for his literal approach to the Greek New Testament, made a stunning observation:

> "The New Testament puts a great deal of emphasis on this second aspect [of salvation]. In the Epistles, the first aspect—justification by faith—is spoken of 19 times, while the second aspect—sanctification —is mentioned 184 times."[5]

Most churches today focus primarily on getting saved but say almost nothing about being transformed. That silence has cost us everything.

Kurath adds:

"Though there are 10 times as many verses in the Epistles addressing the ongoing process of sanctification, the Christian church typically places almost all its emphasis on the one-time event . . . But that's only the beginning. The goal is transformation."[6]

SATAN'S REAL STRATEGY

SATAN DOESN'T NEED to get you into new age or witchcraft to destroy you. He just needs you to settle for a half-gospel. If he can replace transformation with tradition . . . if he can trade relationship for ritual . . . if he can convince you to trust a system instead of a Savior . . . he wins.

Because a transformed heart can't be controlled, and Satan's kingdom is built on control.

THE GOSPEL IS STILL Available

HERE'S THE GOOD NEWS: the solution has already been given. It's:

- Written in the Word of God
- Sealed by the blood of Jesus
- Activated by the Holy Spirit in those willing to surrender everything else

The true Church isn't headquartered in Rome, Geneva, Nashville, or Jerusalem. It's a body of people—Spirit-born, sanctified, and surrendered to Christ.

You don't need permission to be free. You need revelation. And once you see it, you can't unsee it.

A Call to Action

THIS CHAPTER ISN'T JUST theological—it's personal. If you've been trapped in dead religion . . . if you've been taught salvation is a formula or a performance . . . if you're tired of sin management and soul-numbing sermons . . .

There's more.

The real gospel doesn't just pardon sin—it destroys its power. "Forgive, and you will be forgiven" (Luke 6:37). This isn't just moral advice. It's a supernatural trigger. Forgiveness opens the door for sanctification. And sanctification opens the door for everything else — freedom, healing, power, purpose.

Get Ready

IN THE NEXT CHAPTER, we'll begin tracing the roots of Rome's religious machine. You'll see how it was built—why it worked—and how it still survives. But for now, ask yourself:

- Do I know the real Jesus—or just the institutional one?
- Has my heart been transformed—or just catechized?
- Am I walking in the Spirit—or sitting in the pew?

The answers will change your life.

Notes

1. Dave Hunt, *A Woman Rides the Beast* (Eugene, OR: Harvest House Publishers, 1994), 53–57.

2. Philip Schaff, *History of the Christian Church*, vol. 3 (Grand Rapids, MI: Eerdmans, 1910), 29–31.

3. Glenn Sunshine, *Why You Think the Way You Do* (Grand Rapids, MI: Zondervan, 2009), 81–85.

4. D. W. Bercot, *Will the Real Heretics Please Stand Up* (Amberson, PA: Scroll Publishing, 1999), 110–112.

5. Ed Kurath, *Transformation New Testament and Commentary*, Rev. 14 First Printing (Golden, CO: Divinely Designed, 2022), introduction.

6. Ibid.

4

THE LUCIFERIAN LINK

HOW PAGANISM WAS
REBRANDED AS CHRISTIANITY

"Nothing mortal is so unstable and subject to change as power which has no foundation." — Tacitus

"Don't try to base your life on the unstable foundation of human opinions, but instead, build on the unshakable truth of God." — Craig Groeschel

Many people are unaware that the Roman Catholic Church is literally built upon a pagan foundation. Numerous basilicas (early Church buildings) were constructed on top of ancient Roman temples dedicated to false gods. The early Church endured unspeakable persecution under Roman emperors, yet within just a few centuries, the persecutor became the platform—and ultimately the face—of Christianity.

Basilica of San Clemente: Layered in time and purpose—beneath the medieval Basilica of San Clemente lies a 4th-century Christian church, and below that, a Mithraic temple (mithraeum). This physical layering powerfully illustrates the chapter's theme: the Church built atop pagan foundations. See Appendix R for citation.

The institutional structure we know today as the Catholic Church wasn't born from the teachings of Christ but emerged from a politically motivated alliance between religion and empire. The Roman Church adopted many of the same mechanisms of control, hierarchy, and pageantry that defined the very empire that crucified Jesus and slaughtered His followers.

This isn't just a history lesson—it's a spiritual warning.

THE CHURCH'S Foundation in Paganism

THE CHURCH often claims Peter as its foundation, quoting Matthew 16:18: "You are Peter, and on this rock I will build My Church." However, this verse has been mistranslated and misunderstood for centuries. In the original Greek, Jesus uses two distinct words: *petros* (a small stone) and *petra* (a massive bedrock). The Church was never meant to be built on Peter himself, but on the revelation he spoke: that Jesus is the Christ, the Son of the living God.

This mistranslation became the launchpad for the greatest religious empire in human history. And it was no accident.[1]

By claiming Peter as their first "pope" (from the Latin *papa*, meaning "father"), the Vatican sought to legitimize a centralized religious monarchy that Jesus never established. Scripture never refers to Peter as a pope. He was flawed and fallible, denying Christ three times and later being publicly rebuked by Paul for hypocrisy (Galatians 2:11–14). James—not Peter—presided over the Jerusalem council (Acts 15). Paul—not Peter—was the apostle to the Gentiles and the most prolific contributor to New Testament theology.

The Roman Catholic Church's foundation isn't just biblically unsound—it's spiritually dangerous. When your foundation is built on man-made authority, human tradition, and pagan integration, the entire structure becomes a spiritual trap.

THE POLITICAL NECESSITY of Syncretism

WHEN CONSTANTINE I (also known as Constantine the Great) came to power in the early fourth century, he faced a fractured empire and deep religious division. Christianity, once an underground faith, had become impossible to ignore.

Constantine saw an opportunity—not just to unify the empire but to harness the power of religion for political control. His supposed "conversion" in AD 312 was less a spiritual awakening and more a state maneuver. While he legalized Christianity with the Edict of Milan in 313, he never stopped honoring pagan gods—particularly *Sol Invictus*, the unconquered sun.[2]

He repurposed temples, renamed statues, and synchronized the Church calendar with pagan feast days. The result was a hybrid religion, one that allowed pagans and Christians alike to coexist under the imperial banner.

This wasn't reformation. It was assimilation.

The great Arch of Constantine (Rome, 315 AD): Prominently features reused medallions of the sun god Sol and the moon goddess Luna, woven into the newly carved reliefs that praise Constantine. This fusion of pagan solar symbolism and imperial Christian messaging visually reinforces the chapter's main point: political power was deliberately built atop ancient religious traditions. See Appendix R for citation.

The Evolution of Papal Power

CONSTANTINE'S INVOLVEMENT opened the door to ecclesiastical centralization. The bishop of Rome—already influential—gained political status and imperial favor. This escalation laid the foundation for what would become the papacy.

As Rome's influence grew, the bishop of Rome claimed titles and powers far beyond any biblical precedent:

- *Pontifex Maximus* (the supreme priest), a title formerly held by Roman emperors
- *Vicar of Christ*, implying supreme earthly authority
- *Successor of Peter*, built on a misinterpretation of one verse

These titles weren't just spiritual. They were political. And they were designed to consolidate power in the hands of one man.

WHY FOUNDATIONS MATTER

JESUS WARNED us about building on the wrong foundation:

> *"Everyone who hears these words of mine and does not do them will be like a foolish man who built his house on the sand" (Matthew 7:26).*

False Foundation: A powerful visual of the parable's outcome—one house stands firm on rock, untouched by storm; the other collapses into flooding waters. This vividly illustrates Jesus's warning (Matthew 7:26–27) about the fate of spiritual structures built on unstable human traditions instead of Christ. See Appendix R for citation.

The Roman Catholic Church wasn't built upon the apostles' teaching, the Spirit-led gatherings of early Christians, or the freedom of the gospel. It was built upon the remnants of a fallen empire—infused with spiritual deception and cloaked in religious garb.

I'm not attacking sincere Catholics. Many are devoted,

compassionate people. But sincerity doesn't equal truth—a structure can appear impressive yet still be fatally flawed at its foundation.[3]

Conclusion: A False Pillar

THE FOUNDATION of the Catholic Church isn't Jesus Christ. It's a mixture of tradition, political ambition, and spiritual compromise.

The early Church thrived under persecution because it stood on Christ alone. The Roman Church flourished under imperial protection—but it stood on something else. When you build a religion on human legacy, pagan customs, and institutional power, you don't get the body of Christ.

You get Babylon.

Whore of Babylon: A vivid reinterpretation of Hans Burgkmair's 16th-century woodcut, this modern artwork depicts the "Whore of Babylon" as a seductive figure riding the seven-headed beast from Revelation 17. She pours wine from a golden cup—symbolizing spiritual corruption—while occult symbols and ancient empires line the background. This visual reinforces the warning that a global religious empire has been built on power, seduction, and deception. See Appendix R for citation.

Notes

1. Ed Kurath, *Transformation in the Epistles*, rev. ed. (Post Falls, ID: Divinely Designed, 2019), Matthew 16:18 commentary.

2. Alexander Hislop, *The Two Babylons*, 2nd ed. (Ontario, CA: Chick Publications, 1998), 91–94.

3. Philip Schaff, *History of the Christian Church*, vol. 3 (Grand Rapids, MI: Eerdmans, 1910), 85–87.

5

THE PRIESTCRAFT TRAP
RITUAL, POWER, AND THE CULT OF CLERGY

*"For no one can lay any foundation other than the one
already laid, which is Jesus Christ." (1 Corinthians
3:11).*

The Roman Catholic Church claims an unbroken lineage
from the apostle Peter, asserting that Jesus Himself
established Peter as the first pope, granting him
supreme authority over the Church and his successors.

However, if Peter was never appointed pope—and if no such
office was instituted by Christ—then the entire structure of
Roman Catholic authority collapses.

This isn't a minor doctrinal disagreement. It's a seismic revelation that strikes at the heart of Rome's legitimacy.

TRADITION VERSUS SCRIPTURE

. . .

MANY DEVOUT CATHOLICS sincerely believe Peter was chosen to lead the Church. Early Church fathers such as Irenaeus and Tertullian referenced Peter's prominence. Tradition holds that he ministered— and was martyred—in Rome. These traditions later evolved into the doctrine of apostolic succession.

But tradition never overrides revelation. Scripture reveals a very different picture of Peter's role—a man of faith, yes, but also a man of failure, fallibility, and growth.

PETER'S HUMANITY

THE BIBLE DOESN'T PORTRAY Peter as a flawless leader. It shows us a man whose life is defined by zeal and contradiction. Peter was impulsive, rebuking Jesus (Matthew 16:22) and cutting off a man's ear (John 18:10). He denied Christ three times (Luke 22:54–62), and then wept bitterly.

In Antioch, Paul publicly rebuked him for hypocrisy (Galatians 2:11–14). And Peter was married (Mark 1:30), challenging the later Church-imposed celibacy.

Would Jesus entrust the eternal governance of His Church to someone who was repeatedly in need of correction? Or was Christ revealing something much deeper?

WAS PETER THE FIRST POPE?

THE KEY PASSAGE often cited is Matthew 16:18: "You are Peter [Petros], and on this rock [petra] I will build my Church."

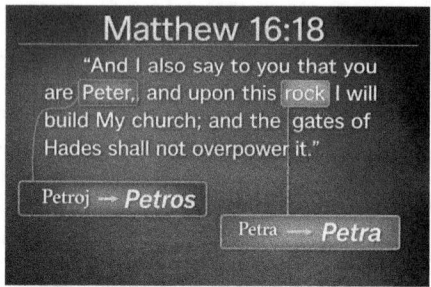

Stone vs. Bedrock: A visual comparison of Petros (Peter, a movable stone) and Petra (Jesus, the bedrock), based on Matthew 16:18. This distinction dismantles the papal foundation myth—Jesus built the Church on truth, not on a man. See Appendix R for citation.

However, the Greek clearly distinguishes between "Peter" and "rock":

- *Petros (πέτρος)* = a small, movable stone.
- *Petra (πέτρα)* = a large, immovable rock or foundation.

Jesus wasn't building His Church on Peter the man—but on Peter's confession two verses earlier that "You are the Christ, the Son of the living God."[1]

Elsewhere in Scripture:

- Christ is the Rock (1 Corinthians 10:4)
- Christ is the Cornerstone (Ephesians 2:20)
- Believers are living stones (1 Peter 2:5)

At no point do the apostles refer to Peter as a pope. Even Peter himself writes, "I am a fellow elder" (1 Peter 5:1)—not a supreme leader.

THE MYTH of Rome and Peter's Bones

. . .

THE CATHOLIC CHURCH asserts that Peter died in Rome and is buried under St. Peter's Basilica. This supposed fact forms the cornerstone of the papacy's claim to divine authority. But Scripture never mentions Peter going to Rome.

Excavation beneath St. Peter's Basilica: Reveals layers of pagan tombs and early Christian burial chambers—highlighting the layered continuity between imperial and religious authority. See Appendix R for citation.

Paul's letter to the Romans (written c. AD 57) never mentions Peter—odd, if he were leading the church there. No New Testament epistle refers to Peter as the bishop of Rome.

Early church records, including those from Clement and Ignatius, honor Peter's martyrdom but don't confirm a Roman episcopacy.[2]

The "bones of Peter" were allegedly discovered during twentieth-century excavations beneath the Vatican. But the evidence is sketchy at best. The bones weren't found in the central tomb. No inscription links them to Peter. The remains were later declared authentic— conveniently—by Pope Paul VI.[3]

(See Appendix N for a more detailed explanation).

. . .

The Rise of Papal Power

THE NOTION of papal supremacy didn't arise during Peter's lifetime. It evolved centuries later, during Rome's transition from persecutor to patron of the Church.

In the fourth and fifth centuries, as the Roman Empire began to collapse, the Bishop of Rome gained both civil authority and spiritual influence. The fusion of imperial politics with Christian leadership transformed bishops into monarchs and the Church into a state religion.

By the time of Leo I (440–461), the doctrine of Petrine primacy was formalized. However, it was built not on the gospel but on Rome's need for continuity, control, and religious centralization.

A Warning from Scripture

PETER HIMSELF WARNED the Church to beware of future deception: "But there were also false prophets among the people, just as there will be false teachers among you. They will secretly introduce destructive heresies" (2 Peter 2:1).

Paul echoed this:

> *"After I depart, savage wolves will come in among you,*
> *not sparing the flock" (Acts 20:29).*

What began as a subtle distortion soon evolved into systemic corruption.

· · ·

CONCLUSION: **Christ Alone**

THE FOUNDATION of the true Church isn't Peter, but Christ. Not tradition. Not succession. Not Rome.

> *"For no one can lay any foundation other than the one already laid, which is Jesus Christ." (1 Corinthians 3:11).*

There is one Rock. One Cornerstone. One Head of the Church. And His name is Jesus.

An early Christian mosaic depicting Christ the Good Shepherd: Symbolically, the cornerstone supporting His flock. This visual ties directly into Ephesians 2:20 and 1 Corinthians 3:11, emphasizing that Christ—not Peter or any human tradition— is the true foundation of the Church. See Appendix R for citation.

Notes

1. Ed Kurath, *Transformation in the Epistles*, rev. ed. (Post Falls, ID: Divinely Designed, 2019), Matthew 16 Greek commentary.

2. D. W. Bercot, *A Dictionary of Early Christian Beliefs* (Peabody, MA: Hendrickson Publishers, 1998), 502–504.

3. Peter de Rosa, *Vicars of Christ: The Dark Side of the Papacy* (New York: Crown Publishing Group, 1988), 27–30.

6

WHEN PHILOSOPHY
REPLACED POWER

HOW GREEK THINKING
HIJACKED THE EARLY CHURCH

*"See to it that no one takes you captive through philos-
ophy and empty deceit, based on human tradition,
based on the elements of the world, rather than
Christ." (Colossians 2:8, CSB).*

C hristianity was never meant to be a system.
      It was born as a supernatural movement—a Spirit-
led revolution that turned the world upside down.

But something happened.

Over time, the church traded its spiritual power for intellectual
prestige. One of the most subtle but dangerous corruptions came
not from emperors or heretics but from philosophers. What began
as a gospel of revelation was slowly hijacked by the gospel of
reason.

THE RISE of Greek Influence

. . .

IN THE FIRST THREE CENTURIES, Christianity was fiercely persecuted.

But after Constantine's rise, Christianity moved from the catacombs to the courtyards of philosophers and aristocrats.

Greek systems, such as Platonism, Stoicism, and Neoplatonism, became the intellectual air of the elite. As the Church gained political favor, its leaders began to absorb and incorporate these ideas in an effort to appear more "respectable" to the elite.

Busts of Plato (left), Socrates (center), and Aristotle (right): Three of the most influential Greek philosophers whose ideas later merged into Church dogma, steering Christianity toward intellectualism and away from Spirit-led truth. See Appendix R for citation.

This shift didn't just affect preaching. It also impacted other aspects of ministry. It redefined the way the Church understood God, salvation, man, and truth itself.

FROM REVELATION to Rationalism

- The Bible began to be interpreted allegorically rather than literally.
- Faith was intellectualized—reduced to assent to creeds rather than union with Christ.

- Sin and salvation were redefined through metaphysical frameworks rather than relational ones.
- God became more like Aristotle's "unmoved mover" than the living God of Abraham.
- The church that once relied on the power of the Spirit now depended on the power of the mind.

Key Figures Who Blended Faith and Philosophy

- **Justin Martyr** called Socrates and Plato "unconscious Christians."[1]
- **Origen** embraced allegory and taught the preexistence of souls—a Platonic concept.[2]
- **Augustine**, deeply influenced by Neoplatonism, introduced deterministic views of salvation that laid the foundation for predestination and original sin as redefined in Western theology.[3]
- **Thomas Aquinas** later fused Aristotelian logic with Church dogma, crafting a system of theology that prioritized philosophical coherence over spiritual revelation.[4]

These men were brilliant—but their brilliance often came at the expense of simplicity and power.

The Legacy of Neoplatonism

. . .

NEOPLATONISM, particularly the teachings of Plotinus, introduced ideas that shaped Catholic mysticism and sacramental theology:

- The material world was viewed as corrupt or inferior.
- Salvation was seen as a mystical ascent—a return to divine unity.
- The divine was increasingly abstract and inaccessible without layers of ritual and hierarchy.

This philosophical dualism infiltrated Christianity, making the spiritual more "holy" than the physical, and making priests, monks, and clergy the gatekeepers to God.

But the New Testament paints a different picture.

Jesus came in the flesh, died in the body, rose in the body, and sent His Spirit to dwell in us—not to institutionalize mystery but to make a relationship with God direct and personal.

PAUL'S **Prophetic Warning**

PAUL SAW THIS INFILTRATION COMING:

> *"See to it that no one takes you captive through philosophy and empty deceit." (Colossians 2:8).*

He wasn't warning against knowledge itself. He was warning against any worldview that replaces Christ with human tradition or abstract speculation.

But the Church didn't listen.

By the Middle Ages, seminaries focused more on training theologians in philosophy than on preparing disciples for power.

Salvation was simplified to formulas. The gospel was filtered through centuries of speculation rather than received through the Word and Spirit.

The Modern Fallout

We still see the effects today:

- Churches that teach theory over transformation.
- Seminaries that graduate philosophers, not shepherds.
- Sermons filled with logic but empty of power.
- Christians who can quote Aquinas but don't know the voice of the Spirit.

What began as the Spirit-led Church of Acts became the academic Church of the West.

And many today still don't know the difference.

George Fox and the Forgotten Reformation

While many recognize Martin Luther and John Calvin as the central figures of the Protestant Reformation, few know of **George Fox**, a spirit-led reformer who emerged a century later with a far more dangerous message: that Christ Himself is the only true teacher, and that every man and woman can hear Him directly.

Fox (1624–1691), founder of the Religious Society of Friends—better known as **Quakers**—was not content to reform the Church of England. He rejected organized religion entirely. He refused to call church buildings "churches," referring to them instead as "steeplehouses." He said God does not dwell in temples made with hands, and he often preached in fields, barns, or open public squares.[5]

Fox believed that any person could minister, regardless of education or gender, if led by the Holy Spirit. He condemned ritualized worship, paid clergy, tithes, and the sacraments of institutional Christianity.[6] Instead, Fox and early Friends gathered in silence—waiting on the Spirit of Christ to speak within.

Fox wrote, "I was to bring people off from all the world's religions, which are in vain."[7] He had no interest in founding another denomination. He simply wanted to restore Christianity to its original simplicity: Christ as head, and the Spirit as teacher.

George Fox preaching beneath an oak tree in colonial Maryland.
His message—Christ alone as teacher, with no need for
steeplehouses, priests, or ritual—challenged both Protestant and
Catholic power structures. He called believers to return to the
original faith: direct, Spirit-led, and unmediated by man. See
Appendix R for citation.

Ed Kurath once wrote, "Fox was a bit like the Apostle Paul, in that George got his theology directly from Jesus."[8] That description could not be more accurate. Fox did not base his convictions on hierarchy, tradition, or interpretation—but on direct revelation through obedient faith.

He testified of an inner voice that said, "There is one, even Christ Jesus, that can speak to thy condition." Fox said that when he heard this, "my heart did leap for joy."[9]

The parallels between Fox's time and ours are striking. Then, as now, religious power structures hated the idea of Spirit-led believers. Fox was imprisoned many times. Entire buildings reportedly shook when he prayed. He was mocked by judges, whipped in public squares, and condemned by both Catholics and Protestants.[10]

But he continued to preach what he had come to know through revelation and experience: that Christ had come to teach His people Himself, and that no mediator was needed but the Light within. This was not mysticism—it was New Testament Christianity.

Fox and the early Quakers believed, as the apostles did, that the gospel was not just to be believed but to be experienced.

It was to transform a person from within—and that transformation was the true mark of salvation.

George Fox belongs not just to the history of the Quakers, but to the history of true Christianity—the kind that obeys God, listens to the Spirit, and refuses to bow to man-made religion.

His legacy is a reminder that Christ has always had a remnant — one that hears His voice and follows no other.

CONCLUSION: **The Mind Must Bow**

THE SOLUTION IS NOT to abandon the mind but to make it bow.

> *"Take every thought captive to obey Christ." (2 Corinthians 10:5).*

Greek philosophy made man the measure of all things.

But true Christianity begins with surrender—with recognizing that God's ways are higher than ours.

Christ is not a concept.

He is a King.

He cannot be systematized.

He must be encountered.

It's time to reclaim the faith that once shook empires—not with arguments, but with power.

Notes

1. D. W. Bercot, *A Dictionary of Early Christian Beliefs* (Peabody, MA: Hendrickson Publishers, 1998), 344.

2. Ibid., 477–478.

3. Dave Hunt, *What Love Is This? Calvinism's Misrepresentation of God* (Bend, OR: The Berean Call, 2002), 103–107.

4. Étienne Gilson, *The Christian Philosophy of St. Thomas Aquinas* (New York: Random House, 1956), 27–35.

5. George Fox, *The Journal of George Fox*, ed. Norman Penney (Cambridge: Cambridge University Press, 1911), accessed July 22, 2025, https://onlinebooks.library.upenn.edu/webbin/book/lookupid?key=olbp42549.

6. Ibid.

7. George Fox, *Journal of George Fox*, rev. ed. of the 1694 Ellwood text (Cambridge: Cambridge University Press, 1952), quoted in Thomas Arnold, *Passages from the Life and Writings of George Fox* (Philadelphia: Friends' Book-Store, ca. 1890).

8. Ed Kurath, email message to the author, May 4, 2021.

9. George Fox, *The Journal of George Fox*, ed. Norman Penney (Cambridge: Cambridge University Press, 1911), 11.

10. *Encyclopaedia Britannica*, s.v. "George Fox," accessed July 22, 2025, https://www.britannica.com/biography/George-Fox.

7

ROMAN PAGANISM GAVE
BIRTH TO CATHOLICISM

THE FUSION OF EMPIRE AND RELIGION
THAT CREATED THE COUNTERFEIT CHURCH

*"You nullify the Word of God by your tradition that you
have handed down. And you do many other similar
things." (Mark 7:13, CSB).*

To understand the true origins of Catholicism, we must
go back, not to the New Testament, but to Rome,
because the Roman Catholic Church isn't built on
Christ. It's built on compromise.

The early Church began in the Spirit. But with the coming of
Constantine, Rome didn't surrender to the gospel—it absorbed it.
And what emerged wasn't a renewed Christianity. It was Christianity rebranded—with the symbols, titles, and rituals of Roman
paganism.

PERSECUTION AND PURITY

. . .

BEFORE THE FLOOD OF CORRUPTION, there was a time of relative purity. The early Church, persecuted by emperors such as Nero, Trajan, and Diocletian, met in secret, shared everything in common, and preached boldly.[1]

They had no temples. No altars. No priestly class. But they had Christ. And under pressure, they thrived.

CONSTANTINE'S COMPROMISE

EVERYTHING CHANGED under Emperor Constantine I. After allegedly seeing a vision of the cross in the sky, he won a key battle and soon legalized Christianity through the Edict of Milan (AD 313).[2] But Constantine didn't convert out of conviction. He never renounced the sun god *Sol Invictus*—he merely merged its worship with Christianity.

Temples became churches. Altars were preserved. Pagan statues were renamed "saints." It was the beginning of a dangerous fusion.

THE PAGAN ROOTS of Catholic Ritual

THE ROMAN EMPIRE didn't lay down its religion. It repackaged it. Even the title *Pontifex Maximus*—used by popes—originally belonged to the high priest of Roman paganism.[3] This wasn't the Church that Christ built. It was an empire in ecclesiastical robes.

Ancient Roman stone inscription featuring "PONT MAX"
(Pontifex Maximus): The title of Rome's highest pagan priest. This
title, deeply rooted in imperial and religious authority, was later
inherited by popes—highlighting the Church's pagan institutional
lineage. See Appendix R for citation.

The Marian Model

THE EXALTATION of Mary in Catholicism closely mirrors pagan mother goddess worship.[4] In Rome, she became the Queen of Heaven—a title God condemns in the Old Testament (Jeremiah 7:18). She was called Co-Redeemer, Mediatrix, and Immaculate, usurping roles clearly given to Christ alone.

Like Isis, Artemis, and Cybele before her, Mary was turned into a divine maternal figure—comforting, commanding, and crowned in gold. The gospel was buried beneath tradition.

THEOLOGICAL CORRUPTION

. . .

WITH PAGAN RITUAL came pagan doctrine. The Mass became a mystical sacrifice. The priesthood reemerged—no longer a priesthood of all believers, but a mediating elite. The Eucharist was deified. Purgatory, indulgences, and penance were added—concepts unknown to the apostles.[5]

The Church that had once preached "It is finished" now taught "Do more." And in doing so, it reversed the message of the cross.

A HISTORY of Blood and Power

THE CHURCH'S embrace of paganism wasn't just spiritual. It became political. The institution that claimed to speak for Christ began to persecute in His name.

The Inquisition tortured those who questioned her teachings.[6] The Crusades were waged with papal blessing. Reformers like Tyndale, Huss, and Savonarola were burned for preaching the gospel.

A 16th-century woodcut depicting the execution of William Tyndale: Strangled and burned for translating the Bible into English. His martyrdom starkly displays the violent edge of the Church's power when it clashed with Scripture and conscience. See Appendix R for citation.

The Church amassed land, power, and political influence unmatched in history. It became the new Rome—in every sense but name.

THE PROTESTANT PROBLEM

THOUGH THE PROTESTANT Reformation exposed many of Rome's errors, it didn't sever every tie. Most Protestant churches still:

- Worship on Sunday, Rome's mandated day
- Celebrate pagan-rooted holidays
- Retain hierarchical structures rooted in Rome
- Follow seminary models built on Greco-Roman educational ideals

Because the Reformation was incomplete, Rome's echo still lingers in pews around the world.

. . .

Conclusion: **Come Out of Her**

GOD NEVER CALLED His people to blend in with Babylon. He called them out:

> *"Come out of her, My people, so that you will not share in her sins." (Revelation 18:4).*

The Roman Catholic Church isn't a slow drift from truth. It's a wholesale rebranding of paganism—cloaked in religious vocabulary and Christian symbols. The call is the same now as it was then: repent, come out, and return to Christ.

Notes

1. Philip Schaff, *History of the Christian Church*, vol. 2 (Grand Rapids, MI: Eerdmans, 1910), 48–50.

2. Glenn Sunshine, *Why You Think the Way You Do* (Grand Rapids, MI: Zondervan, 2009), 87–88.

3. Alexander Hislop, *The Two Babylons*, 2nd ed. (Ontario, CA: Chick Publications, 1998), 96–101.

4. Dave Hunt, *A Woman Rides the Beast* (Eugene, OR: Harvest House Publishers, 1994), 102–105.

5. Ralph Woodrow, *Babylon Mystery Religion* (Riverside, CA: Woodrow Evangelistic Association, 1966), 121–124.

6. D. W. Bercot, *Will the Real Heretics Please Stand Up* (Amberson, PA: Scroll Publishing, 1999), 102.

8

HOW EMPEROR CONSTANTINE CORRUPTED CHRISTIANITY

THE POLITICAL TROJAN HORSE THAT HIJACKED THE GOSPEL

"If the light within you is darkness—how great is that darkness!" (Matthew 6:23).

I f Satan couldn't destroy the early Church through persecution, he would corrupt it through power. And he found the perfect instrument in Emperor Constantine.

Constantine's so-called "conversion" didn't purify Rome. It paved the way for Rome to infiltrate the Church—permanently altering Christian history. What emerged wasn't the kingdom of God. It was a counterfeit empire with a Christian face.

CONSTANTINE'S STRATEGIC Conversion

ACCORDING TO LEGEND, Constantine experienced a vision before the Battle of the Milvian Bridge in AD 312. He reportedly saw a cross in the sky with the words "In this sign, conquer." He ordered his soldiers to mark their shields with the Christian symbol, won the battle, and soon after legalized Christianity through the Edict of Milan (AD 313).

But was it a true conversion—or a calculated political maneuver?

The fruit reveals the truth: Constantine continued minting coins bearing the image of Sol Invictus, the sun god.[1] He was baptized only on his deathbed by an Arian bishop, and Arianism was condemned as heretical.[2] He executed his wife and son years after declaring himself to be a Christian.[3]

This wasn't spiritual rebirth. It was political opportunism.

THE MERGER of Paganism and Christianity

CONSTANTINE DIDN'T PURGE PAGANISM. He blended it with Christianity:

- He mandated Sunday worship in honor of the sun god.
- He synchronized Christmas with the birth of Sol Invictus (December 25).
- He aligned Easter with pagan spring fertility rites.
- He converted pagan temples into churches and rebranded statues of gods as "saints."[4]

This merger created a religion that bore Christ's name—but not His Spirit. The Church that had once stood against the empire was now consumed by it.

THE COUNCIL OF NICAEA: Unity or Control?

. . .

IN AD 325, Constantine convened the Council of Nicaea, often hailed as a milestone in Christian theology. The council affirmed key doctrines, such as the deity of Christ. But it also established a precedent that would echo for centuries: theology was now enforced by imperial decree.

An 18th-century depiction of the Council of Nicaea (AD 325):
Bishops gathered under imperial oversight, with Constantine's
influence unmistakable. Theology became law that day, marking a
shift from Spirit-led truth to state-enforced doctrine. See Appendix
R for citation.

Constantine did not serve as a theologian, but he presided ceremonially over the gathering and strongly pressed for unity across the empire.[5] Bishops who refused to sign the creed were pressured, marginalized, or exiled.[6]

Imperial authority now stood behind ecclesiastical decisions, creating what historians describe as a new partnership between throne and altar.[7] For the first time in Christian history, theological conclusions carried the backing of state power. That precedent would echo for centuries.

THE SWORD of the State

CONSTANTINE DIDN'T JUST WANT unity—he wanted control. Those who opposed the Council of Nicaea's decisions were:

- Removed from office
- Banished from cities
- Labeled heretics

It was no longer just about truth. It was about enforcement. The Church that had survived Rome's sword had now picked it up.

SYMBOLS OF APOSTASY

THE SYMBOLISM CONSTANTINE introduced remains with us today:

- Halos: borrowed from depictions of sun gods.
- Obelisks: pagan symbols of sun worship—now displayed in Vatican Square.
- The crux quadrata (equal-armed cross): used by Constantine but never described in the New Testament.[7]

The 4,000-year-old Egyptian obelisk: Imported from the Circus of Nero, now stands at the center of St. Peter's Square, topped by a cross. Originally a pagan solar monument, it was re-erected by Pope Sixtus V and later crowned with Christian symbols—powerfully illustrating how imperial religion replaced biblical faith with syncretized iconography. See Appendix R for citation.

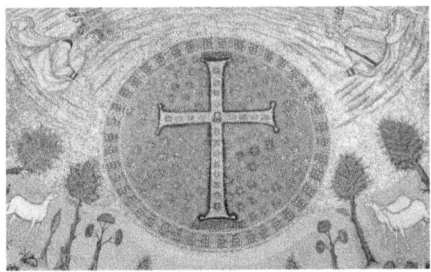

A crux quadrata (Greek cross) with four equal arms: This symbol became prominent after Constantine's reign. It reflects an imperial, systemic Christianity rather than the salvific, cruciform faith of the New Testament. See Appendix R for citation.

The True Cost of Constantine's Influence

BY JOINING WITH ROME, the Church lost its identity. It ceased to be the persecuted Bride. It became the imperial counterfeit. It traded the power of the Spirit for the privileges of empire. It was no longer a living Body—it was an institution.

By the fourth century, Christianity had become "victorious." But it was no longer Christian.

. . .

THE MODERN FALLOUT

CONSTANTINE'S COMPROMISE still shapes Christianity today:

- Sunday worship enforced by tradition, not Scripture (see Acts 20:7).
- Pagan holidays embraced and rebranded. Clergy robes and rituals copied from the Roman hierarchy.
- Church–state alliances that favor comfort over conviction.

And few believers question it. But Jesus warned, "If the light within you is darkness—how great is that darkness!" (Matthew 6:23).

CONCLUSION: Expose and Escape

CONSTANTINE'S LEGACY isn't a Christian victory. It's Christian surrender. He didn't conquer for Christ. He conquered Christianity itself—twisting it into something imperial, structured, and unrecognizable. The system he helped create—Roman Catholicism—would go on to persecute, deceive, and enslave millions.

The call remains: "Come out of her" (Revelation 18:4). Reject the empire of lies. Return to the simplicity of the gospel. Return to the power of the Spirit. Return to Jesus Christ.

Notes

1. Alexander Hislop, *The Two Babylons*, 2nd ed. (Ontario, CA: Chick Publications, 1998), 91–94.

2. Dave Hunt, *A Woman Rides the Beast* (Eugene, OR: Harvest House Publishers, 1994), 53.

3. Peter de Rosa, *Vicars of Christ: The Dark Side of the Papacy* (New York: Crown Publishing Group, 1988), 19–20.

4. I. A. Sadler, *Mystery Babylon the Great: The Church of Rome and the European Union Exposed to the Light of Truth* (Reading, UK: I. A. Sadler, 2002), 75–78.

5. H. A. Drake, *Constantine and the Bishops: The Politics of Intolerance* (Baltimore: Johns Hopkins University Press, 2000), 200–215.

6. William Webster, *The Church of Rome at the Bar of History* (Edinburgh: Banner of Truth Trust, 1995), 43–46.

7. Walter Veith, *Truth Matters* (Ontario, Canada: Amazing Discoveries, 2002), 181–182.

PART II

THE SYSTEM

HOW IT CONTINUES TODAY

9

THE VATICAN'S GLOBAL AGENDA

HOW ROME SEEKS TO RECLAIM RELIGIOUS RULE OVER THE EARTH

"Come, I will show you the judgment of the great harlot who sits on many waters ... With her the kings of the earth committed adultery, and the inhabitants of the earth were intoxicated with the wine of her adulteries." (Revelation 17:1–2).

There is a system in place today—political, religious, and economic—that most people mistake for Christianity. It wears a cross. It quotes Scripture. It claims to be the Church Jesus founded. But it's none of those things.

It's a counterfeit. It's a system of control. And it's preparing the world for the final deception foretold in the book of Revelation. At the center of it all sits the Vatican.

A POLITICAL POWER in Religious Clothing

. . .

UNLIKE ANY OTHER RELIGIOUS INSTITUTION, the Vatican isn't just a church—it's a sovereign nation with embassies, political alliances, intelligence networks, and financial influence across the globe.

A group portrait of Vatican and Italian leaders just before signing the 1929 Lateran Treaty: Including Benito Mussolini and Cardinal Pietro Gasparri. This historic agreement established the Vatican as a sovereign state and officially merged religious authority with political power. See Appendix R for citation.

The Vatican City State was established in 1929 through the Lateran Treaty, signed by Benito Mussolini and Pope Pius XI.[1] This agreement gave the pope civil authority over a nation, not just a denomination. The pope became both a spiritual monarch and a head of state.

MORE THAN A RELIGION

THE VATICAN HAS LONG POSITIONED itself as a mediator between world powers:

- It helped broker the Helsinki Accords during the Cold War.

- It maintained diplomatic relations with both the Nazis and the Allies during World War II.
- It played a documented role in postwar European integration efforts and diplomatic unification initiatives.[2]

While presenting itself as a peace-making institution, the Vatican's reach has often been used to prop up regimes, conceal war crimes, and protect clergy guilty of abuse. As journalist Avro Manhattan wrote, "The Catholic Church isn't only a spiritual organization—it is a political one. Its hierarchy is intertwined with the governing systems of the world."[3]

THE VATICAN'S Ecumenical Strategy

IN RECENT DECADES, Rome has launched a global campaign for unity —but unity on its own terms. At the heart of this campaign is ecumenism, a religious movement that seeks to bring together Protestants, Eastern Orthodox, Jews, Muslims, and other faiths under a single spiritual umbrella.

A tour guide points to the bronze memorial engraving
commemorating the 1986 World Day of Prayer for Peace in Assisi:
Where Pope John Paul II gathered religious leaders from across the
globe, including Buddhists, Muslims, Hindus, and tribal faiths. This
historic event signified the Vatican's attempt to position itself as the
central moral authority over a unified global faith. See Appendix R
for citation.

In 1986, Pope John Paul II hosted the Assisi interfaith summit, where Buddhists, Hindus, and even tribal shamans were invited to pray alongside Catholics on equal footing.[4]

The Second Vatican Council (1962–1965) redefined the Church's relationship with non-Catholic Christians and other religions, calling Muslims "those who adore the one God."[5] In 2019, Pope Francis signed the *Document on Human Fraternity* with Sheikh Ahmed elTayeb, promoting a common global faith rooted in "love" rather than truth.[6]

Pope Francis (left) and Sheikh Ahmed el-Tayeb (right): Sign the Document on Human Fraternity for World Peace and Living Together in Abu Dhabi, February 2019. This landmark agreement reflects the Vatican's ecumenical ambition to unite all religions under a common moral framework—precisely the global spiritual system critiqued in Revelation 17. See Appendix R for citation.

But beneath the smiles and olive branches lies the Vatican's longstanding belief that all roads must ultimately lead back to Rome.

THE JESUIT ENGINE

MUCH OF THE Vatican's behind-the-scenes activity has been orchestrated by the Jesuits, an elite Catholic order founded in 1540 by Ignatius of Loyola. Their stated mission is to "go anywhere and do anything" in service of the pope. Historically, the Jesuits were:

- Banned from multiple European countries for political interference
- Linked to assassination plots, revolutions, and propaganda campaigns
- Masters of education, infiltration, and high-level diplomacy[7]

Jesuit-run universities—including *Georgetown*, *Fordham*, and

Boston College—have produced presidents, diplomats, intelligence agents, and thought leaders who shape Western policy. Their network has quietly permeated academia, government, and media.

Pope Francis was the first Jesuit pope—a signal that the order had not only survived but taken the throne.

The official Jesuit seal: Featuring the IHS monogram within a radiant sunburst—has symbolized the Society of Jesus' deep allegiance to the papacy since the 16th century. This emblem represents Rome's religious, educational, and political reach, now woven into the heraldry of Pope Francis, the first Jesuit pope. See Appendix R for citation.

Mystery Babylon Revealed

THE BOOK of Revelation describes a woman clothed in scarlet and purple, drunk with the blood of saints, seated on a beast with seven heads and ten horns:

> *"The woman you saw is that great city that reigns over the kings of the earth." (Revelation 17:18).*

This isn't a mere metaphor—the Vatican matches this description with haunting precision:

- Scarlet and purple are the colors of Catholic cardinals and bishops.
- It's seated on seven hills—the ancient city of Rome.
- It claims to reign over kings through its diplomatic corps.
- It's intoxicated with power, wealth, and blasphemy.

The prophetic imagery of Revelation 17 has led many interpreters to identify Rome as the archetype of this system that seduces the nations with false religion and spiritual authority.

A procession of Catholic bishops and clergy: Featuring scarlet, purple, and gold vestments—during the ordination of Fülöp Kocsis, bishop of Hajdúdorog. These colors mirror the prophetic imagery of Revelation 17's "great harlot," clothed in royal splendor and seated atop worldly power. See Appendix R for citation.

A Counterfeit Bride

THE ROMAN CATHOLIC CHURCH claims to be the Bride of Christ. But Scripture tells a different story.

The true Bride is washed in the blood of the Lamb—not the traditions of men. The true Church is led by the Spirit—not the Vatican. The true faith is built on Christ alone—not on priests, popes, or sacraments.

Rome has usurped the gospel with another gospel. It has replaced the simplicity of the cross with the spectacle of religion. And through this system, Satan prepares the world for his final deception.

THE NARROW PATH Remains

THE GOOD NEWS IS THIS: Jesus is still calling His people out of deception:

> *"Come out of her, My people, so that you will not share in her sins." (Revelation 18:4).*

This isn't just a call to leave the Catholic Church. It's a call to leave every system that replaces Christ with control. It's a call to be cleansed by grace—not works. To walk by the Spirit—not sacraments. To know God—not just perform for Him.

Notes

1. John Cornwell, *Hitler's Pope: The Secret History of Pius XII* (New York: Viking, 1999), 26–29.

2. Avro Manhattan, *The Vatican Billions* (Ontario, CA: Chick Publications, 1983), 85–87.

3. Manhattan, *The Vatican Billions*, 33.

4. Dave Hunt, *A Woman Rides the Beast* (Eugene, OR: Harvest House Publishers, 1994), 401–405.

5. Second Vatican Council, *Nostra Aetate* (Declaration on the Relation of the Church to Non-Christian Religions), October 28, 1965, para. 3.

6. "Document on Human Fraternity for World Peace and Living Together," Vatican.va, February 4, 2019, https://www.vatican.va.

7. Eric Jon Phelps, *Vatican Assassins* (Lowell, MI: Lowvehm Publishing, 2001), 105–122.

10

BLASPHEMIES OF THE ROMAN CHURCH
HOW THE POPE, THE MASS, AND MARY REPLACE CHRIST

"Who is like the beast? Who is able to wage war against it?" (Revelation 13:4).

Blasphemy isn't just profanity. According to Scripture, it's far more specific:

- Claiming to be God (John 10:33)
- Claiming to forgive sins (Mark 2:7)
- Corrupting true worship (Ezekiel 20:27–28)

By these definitions, the Roman Catholic Church is steeped in blasphemy—not by accident, but by design. It has exalted man over God, tradition over truth, and ceremony over Spirit. And it does so in the name of Christ.

THE POPE: A Man Who Claims to Be God

"We hold upon this earth the place of God Almighty." — Pope Leo XIII[1]

A JULY 13, 1895, report in the Swiss Catholic newspaper *Le Catholique National* attributed to Cardinal Giuseppe Sarto (later Pope Pius X) language that critics argue blurs the line between representation and divine identity.[2]

The ornate papal tiara and ceremonial stole used in pre–Vatican II papal coronations: Symbols of pontifical authority and elevation above all earthly rulers. These lavish regalia reinforced papal claims of divine status, aligning with statements from Popes Leo XIII and Pius X that the pope holds the place of God on earth. See Appendix R for citation.

Statements attributed to past pontiffs and Catholic publications have described the papal office in terms that verge on divine representation. They're official declarations from Rome's highest office. Yet Scripture is clear: "I am the Lord; that is My name, and I will not give My glory to another" (Isaiah 42:8). To claim divine titles isn't authority. It's blasphemy.

· · ·

Forgiveness For Sale

Catholic priests claim the power to forgive sins, citing John 20:23. However, Jesus gave this commission to the apostles collectively after they received the Holy Spirit, not to establish a future priesthood. Nowhere in Scripture do we find:

- Confession to a priest
- Assigned penance
- Indulgences
- "Time off" purgatory

A wooden confessional inside the Chapel of Saint Anne (France):
Illustrates the institutionalization of priest-mediated absolution
within Roman Catholic practice. The confessional system
formalized a model of forgiveness that placed clerical authority
between the believer and God—contrasting with the New
Testament teaching that forgiveness and reconciliation come
directly through Jesus Christ (1 Timothy 2:5; Hebrews 4:16). See
Appendix R for citation.

These are man-made systems—tools of guilt manipulation and institutional control. Selling indulgences wasn't a medieval fluke; it was a systemic practice—and it continues today in subtler forms.

"There is one mediator between God and men—the man Christ Jesus." (1 Timothy 2:5).

THE MASS: A Daily Crucifixion?

. . .

THE CATHOLIC MASS teaches that Christ is re-presented daily as a living sacrifice: "The same Christ who offered Himself once... is offered in the Eucharist" (Catechism of the Catholic Church §1367).[3]

Pope Benedict XVI elevates the consecrated Host during Mass: Visually depicting Rome's belief in the 're-sacrifice' of Christ, a practice you identify as blasphemous compared to Hebrews 10:10–12. See Appendix R for citation.

They believe:

- The bread and wine literally become Christ's flesh and blood
- His sacrifice is renewed at every Mass
- Priests can summon His presence at will

But Scripture says:

"Christ was offered once to bear the sins of many."
(Hebrews 9:28).

"It is finished." (John 19:30).

Re-sacrificing Christ isn't reverent. It's blasphemous.

MARY: **The Queen of Heaven?**

ROME CLAIMS it doesn't worship Mary. But her titles betray that claim:

- Mediatrix of all graces
- Co-Redemptrix
- Queen of Heaven[4]

Catholics pray to her. Nations are consecrated to her. Churches are built in her honor. This isn't biblical honor—it's pagan elevation.

The title "Queen of Heaven" appears in Scripture only as a pagan goddess, condemned by God:

Madonna and Child Enthroned with Angels: *Workshop of Bernardino Luini (c. early 16th century). This Renaissance depiction reflects the development of Marian enthronement imagery within late medieval and early modern Catholic art, portraying Mary as a regal, mediating figure seated above the faithful. Such visual theology parallels the Church's growing emphasis on Marian intercession and queenship—concepts that extend beyond the New Testament's presentation of Mary as a humble servant of God (Luke 1:38). See Appendix R for citation.*

"Do you not see what they are doing... pouring out drink offerings to the Queen of Heaven?" (Jeremiah 7:18).

THE ULTIMATE BLASPHEMY: Replacing Christ

· · ·

ROME's greatest offense isn't one doctrine. It's the structure-wide substitution of Christ Himself:

- His blood replaced by sacraments
- His intercession replaced by Mary and the saints
- His authority replaced by the pope
- His finished work replaced by rituals

This isn't biblical faith. It's spiritual Babylon.

ED KURATH on False Mediators

"THE SPIRIT of religion is Satan's most subtle deception. It keeps people near the truth, but without transformation."[5]

Kurath describes how religious systems construct elaborate scaffolding that appears to be Christian, but replaces the Person of Christ with structures of dead works. Catholicism is perhaps the most powerful version of that deception.

THE SPIRIT of Antichrist

> "He will oppose and exalt himself above every so-called god or object of worship, so that he sits in God's temple, proclaiming himself to be God." (2 Thessalonians 2:4).

Detail from The Preaching and Deeds of the Antichrist (c. 1500–1504) by Luca Signorelli: Located in the San Brizio Chapel of Orvieto Cathedral. A Christ-like figure, subtly distorted, is manipulated by a demonic entity whispering into his ear—representing a counterfeit messiah figure empowered by Satan and speaking blasphemies in God's name. See Appendix R for citation.

THIS VERSE DOESN'T DESCRIBE ONLY one man. It describes a system — one that exalts a human vicar, replaces Christ, demands worship, performs signs and wonders, and deceives millions.

This isn't hyperbole. It's prophecy—fulfilled in plain sight.

CONCLUSION: Call It What It Is

THE ROMAN CATHOLIC CHURCH BLASPHEMIES:

- The Father by exalting man
- The Son by re-sacrificing Him

- The Spirit, by building a machine that denies His power

It's not a Christian denomination with flaws. It's a religious empire dressed in Christian language—a spiritual counterfeit.

> *"They exchanged the truth of God for a lie, and worshiped and served what has been created instead of the Creator." (Romans 1:25).*

Notes

1. Leo XIII, *Praeclara Gratulationis Publicae* (On the Reunion of Christendom), encyclical letter, June 20, 1894.

2. Cardinal Giuseppe Sarto (later Pope Pius X), sermon as reported in *Le Catholique National* (Bern, Switzerland), July 13, 1895. The wording is preserved in later Protestant polemical literature; the original French publication reflects contemporary ultramontane views of papal representation.

3. Catechism of the Catholic Church, 2nd ed. (Vatican City: Libreria Editrice Vaticana, 1997), §1367.

4. I. A. Sadler, *Mystery Babylon the Great: The Church of Rome and the European Union Exposed to the Light of Truth* (Reading, UK: I. A. Sadler, 2002), 91–94.

5. Ed Kurath, *I Will Give You Rest* (Post Falls, ID: Divinely Designed, 2003), chap. 7.

11

DO CATHOLICS WORSHIP MARY ABOVE JESUS?

THE QUEEN OF HEAVEN VERSUS THE GOSPEL OF CHRIST

"They have made her into a goddess without the name." — Dave Hunt

A sk any devout Catholic if they worship Mary, and the answer will be immediate: "No. We venerate her."

But look past the terminology . . . Past the candles, the shrines, the prayers, the processions . . . And you'll find a woman who's quietly replaced her Son. This isn't biblical honor. This is spiritual idolatry.

WHAT THE CHURCH Teaches

THE CATHOLIC CATECHISM SAYS:

"Mary is honored with the title 'Mother of God,' to whose protection the faithful fly in all their dangers and needs."[1]

"This motherhood of Mary in the order of grace continues

uninterruptedly . . . until the eternal fulfillment of all the elect."[2] According to Rome, Mary:

- Was conceived without sin (Immaculate Conception)
- Was taken bodily into heaven (Assumption)
- Intercedes continually
- Dispenses grace
- Is Queen of Heaven

These aren't fringe beliefs. They're official Catholic dogma. But none of this comes from Scripture.

THE REALITY of Devotion

IN PRACTICE:

- Many Catholics pray more to Mary than to Jesus
- The Rosary contains 53 Hail Marys and only 6 Our Fathers
- Shrines to Mary far outnumber those to Christ
- Marian feast days and titles fill the liturgical calendar

Statues of Our Lady of Grace (Miraculous Medal), Philippines:
Multiple statues of Our Lady of Grace, the Marian figure associated
with the Miraculous Medal devotion, are displayed in public
devotional settings in the Philippines. The imagery reflects the
global spread and localization of Marian devotion originating from
19th-century France, emphasizing Mary as a channel of grace and
intercessory power. This visual repetition illustrates how the
symbolism of the Miraculous Medal—rays of grace, Marian
mediation, and devotional posture—has been replicated worldwide
in modern Catholic devotional practice. See Appendix R for citation.

In many cultures, nations are consecrated to Mary rather than to Jesus. She is called:

- Advocate
- Co-Redemptrix
- Mediatrix of all graces

This isn't "veneration." It's worship by every biblical standard.

A 1518 engraving by Albrecht Dürer titled Virgin Mary Crowned by Two Angels: Mary gently cradles the Christ-child as angels descend to place a crown upon her head—visually exalting her above her biblical role. This portrayal reinforces how Catholic tradition has elevated Mary into a near-divine status, despite Scripture's clarity that Christ alone is crowned above all. See Appendix R for citation.

What Scripture Says About Mary

MARY WAS FAITHFUL, obedient, and honored. But never exalted.

"Blessed are you among women." (Luke 1:42).

"Do whatever He tells you." (John 2:5).

Those were her words. And her final appearance in Scripture points—not to herself—but to Christ.

When a woman praised Mary publicly, Jesus replied:

"Blessed rather are those who hear the word of God and obey it." (Luke 11:28).

Jesus never elevated Mary. He redirected attention away from bloodlines and toward obedience.

Pagan Parallels

THE VENERATION of a divine mother isn't unique to Catholicism. It's also found in:

- Babylon: Semiramis and Tammuz
- Egypt: Isis and Horus
- Greece: Aphrodite and Eros
- Rome: Venus and Cupid

Isis Nursing Horus: *Ancient Egyptian depiction of the goddess Isis nursing her son Horus, a maternal iconography that symbolized divine motherhood, protection, and royal legitimacy in pagan religion. This motif predates Christianity by more than a millennium and appears widely across Egyptian religious art. See Appendix R for citation.*

Virgin Nursing the Christ Child (Virgo Lactans): *Tempera on panel, 14th century. Medieval depiction of Mary nursing the infant Jesus, a devotional image type known as* Virgo Lactans. *This form became popular in late medieval Christianity and visually parallels earlier pagan mother-and-child imagery used to communicate nurture, intercession, and sacred motherhood. See Appendix R for citation.*

Every pagan religion glorifies the feminine as divine. Catholicism simply repackaged the archetype—and called her Mary.[3] This explains:

- The "Queen of Heaven" title (Jeremiah 44:17)
- Maternal imagery in art
- Marian apparitions across the world
- Worship disguised as devotion

THE DECEPTION of Marian Apparitions

FROM FATIMA to Lourdes to Medjugorje, visions of Mary have become a global phenomenon. These apparitions:

- Deliver new messages
- Demand devotion
- Promise salvation through her heart
- Threaten judgment on those who reject her

Consider Fatima: "To save them, God wishes to establish in the world devotion to my Immaculate Heart."[4]

That's not the gospel. It's religious coercion.

A marble statue of the Virgin of Fátima: Carved by Portuguese sculptor José Ferreira Thedim in 1920, originally donated to the Diocese of Leiria. Modeled after descriptions from the Marian apparitions at Fátima, this crowned image became an object of widespread veneration and pilgrimage—illustrating how Catholic devotion can drift from reverence to religious idolatry. See Appendix R for full citation.

"Even Satan disguises himself as an angel of light." (2 Corinthians 11:14).

These messages contradict Scripture. They elevate Mary above Christ.

ED KURATH: When Devotion Becomes Deception

. . .

Ed Kurath warned, "Satan doesn't mind if you believe in Jesus—as long as He's not your first love."[5]

Many Catholics love Mary deeply. But that love becomes a replacement—not a reflection—of love for Christ. That is idolatry.

The Real Cost

This isn't about semantics. It's about salvation. If you:

- Trust Mary's intercession over Christ's
- Obey apparitions over the Word
- Pray to Mary instead of the Father through the Son

You've embraced another gospel:

> *"Even if we or an angel from heaven should preach a
> gospel other than the one we preached . . . let them
> be under God's curse." (Galatians 1:8).*

The Real Mary

The True Mary would weep at the idolatry done in her name. She never asked for a crown. She never accepted worship.

She'd say today what she said then: Worship Jesus. Trust Jesus. Follow Jesus.

Anything more than that isn't honor. It's blasphemy:

"Worship the Lord your God, and serve Him only."
(Matthew 4:10).

Notes

1. Catechism of the Catholic Church, 2nd ed. (Vatican City: Libreria Editrice Vaticana, 1997), §971.

2. Catechism of the Catholic Church, 2nd ed. (Vatican City: Libreria Editrice Vaticana, 1997), §969.

3. Alexander Hislop, *The Two Babylons*, 2nd ed. (Ontario, CA: Chick Publications, 1998), 95–99.

4. Congregation for the Doctrine of the Faith, *The Message of Fatima* (Vatican City: Libreria Editrice Vaticana, 2000), https://www.vatican.va.

5. Ed Kurath, *I Will Give You Rest* (Post Falls, ID: Divinely Designed, 2003), chap. 6.

12

CORRUPT POPES:
ROME'S ROTTEN FRUIT

SEX, SORCERY, AND THE DARK
HISTORY OF PAPAL RULE

"By their fruit you will recognize them." (Matthew 7:16).

The Roman Catholic Church claims to be the one true Church, founded by Jesus Christ and led by an unbroken succession of holy men—popes—who serve as the vicar of Christ on Earth.

But history tells a much darker story.

The list of corrupt, depraved, and morally bankrupt popes is long and disturbing. These men were not shepherds of Christ's flock. They were tyrants, sexual deviants, warmongers, occultists —even atheists. Some ran crime syndicates from inside the Vatican.

If the papacy were established by Jesus, would He have handed His Church to men like this?

The altar and central nave of St. Peter's Basilica shimmer with gold, marble, and imperial ornamentation: Testifying not to the poverty of Christ, but to the wealth and power accumulated by Rome. This grand cathedral stands as the crown jewel of a religious system that once martyred the early Church, then absorbed its image to rule in its place. See Appendix R for full citation.

The Pope Isn't the Rock

WE'VE ALREADY DISMANTLED the myth that Peter was the first pope or that the pope is the "rock" upon which Christ built His Church. That falsehood was the Vatican's original power grab.

However, once the Church consolidated its political power during the Dark Ages and the Inquisition, the papacy shifted from spiritual authority to imperial dominance. And what followed was centuries of moral collapse.

HISTORICAL ACCOUNTS of Papal Evil

THE FOLLOWING examples are not Protestant slander. They're documented by Catholic historians and former clergy.

- **Pope Sergius III** (904–911): Murdered his predecessor and fathered a child with his teenage mistress.
- **Pope John XII** (955–964): Turned the Lateran Palace into a brothel, toasted the Devil during mass, and died in bed with a married woman.[1]

IOANNES·XII·PP·ROMANVS

Pope John XII (r. 955–964): Born Octavianus of Tusculum, is infamous for being one of the most depraved men to occupy the papal office. Historical accounts allege he turned the Lateran Palace into a brothel, invoked the devil during Mass, and died while committing adultery. His reign epitomizes the Saeculum Obscurum —a "dark age" of papal corruption known as the Pornocracy. See Appendix R for full citation.

- **Pope Benedict IX** (1032–1048): Elected pope as a teen, sold the office for gold, and later reclaimed it by force.[2]
- **Pope Alexander VI** (1492–1503): Fathered multiple children with mistresses, held orgies in the Vatican, and bribed his way into power.[3]
- **Pope Leo X** (1513–1521): Mocked the gospel and

famously said, "It has served us well, this myth of Christ."[4]

If the papacy is divinely appointed, how did such men ascend to that office?

THE PORNOCRACY and Noble Puppets

THE TENTH-CENTURY PAPACY is known by historians as the **Pornocracy** —a time when the papal throne was dominated by powerful Roman noblewomen. Marozia and her family installed popes as lovers and political pawns.

During this period:

- Popes were poisoned, strangled, or ousted
- The throne was bought, sold, or inherited
- Morality vanished behind Vatican walls[5]

An early 19th-century engraving, likely based on medieval descriptions, depicting Marozia of Tusculum (c. 890–937): The senatrix of Rome and political matriarch who installed, manipulated, or mothered multiple popes during the Saeculum Obscurum, also known as the Pornocracy. Her shadow over the papacy illustrates how secular and immoral forces have long shaped Rome's religious leadership, utterly undermining the claim to apostolic succession or divine appointment. See Appendix R for full citation.

Relic Worship and Death Fetishism

THE CATHOLIC OBSESSIONS WITH BONES, skulls, and body parts of "saints" aren't biblical—it's necromantic:

- Mummified hands are encased in altars
- Blood vials are paraded through the streets
- Glass coffins display corpses for adoration

Scripture warns:

> *"Do not consult the dead or practice divination."*
> *(Deuteronomy 18:10–11).*

Yet popes kiss relics and build shrines to them. This isn't honor. It's idolatry.

Relic Veneration: Displayed in ornate regalia, this bejeweled corpse exemplifies the Catholic practice of relic veneration—where the remains of saints are adorned with gold, encased in glass, and honored as sacred. While presented as reverence, such rituals blur the line between commemoration and death worship, echoing pagan practices forbidden in Scripture. See Appendix R for full citation.

Transubstantiation and the Repeated Sacrifice

PERHAPS THE MOST THEOLOGICALLY OFFENSIVE practice is the Mass —specifically, the teaching of **transubstantiation**, which claims the wafer becomes the literal flesh of Christ.

Every day, Catholic priests "re-present" Jesus in the Eucharist as a new sacrifice. They describe this as the "unbloody sacrifice."

This isn't reverence—it's ritual cannibalism cloaked in mystery.

> *"We have been made holy through the sacrifice of the body of Jesus Christ once for all." (Hebrews 10:10).*

> *"It is finished." (John 19:30).*

To re-crucify Christ daily isn't devotion. It's blasphemy.

. . .

Occultism and Satanic Infiltration

While some popes dabbled in the occult, others were openly associated with demonic practices:

- **Pope Sylvester II** (999–1003): Linked to magical devices and necromantic texts
- **Pope Honorius III** (1216–1227): Associated with the *Grimoire of Honorius*, used in satanic rituals

A 1720 woodcut depicting witches presenting wax dolls to the devil: A classic portrayal of early-modern beliefs about satanic ritual and spiritual corruption. Hooded figures, symbolic gestures, and infernal themes highlight how ritual magic was historically feared and condemned. Though not Vatican-specific, this image visually supports claims of ritualistic perversion within religious institutions, especially those accused of blending spiritual power with occult ceremony. See Appendix R for full citation.

- **Pope Paul VI** (1963–1978): Admitted, "The smoke of Satan has entered the Church"[6]

Some Catholic critics and former insiders have alleged:

- Luciferian black masses

- Blood rituals
- Allegiance to ancient spiritual darkness[7]

> *"He will exalt himself . . . and sit in God's temple,*
> *proclaiming himself to be God." (2 Thessalonians*
> *2:4).*

While this passage may ultimately refer to the Antichrist, the spirit behind it already inhabits the system.

CONTROLLED OPPOSITION: **The Illusion of Reform**

MODERN POPES APPEAR humble and pastoral. But the system is unchanged:

- The pope still claims infallibility
- The Vatican remains a sovereign nation
- The cult of Mary, relics, and the Eucharist continues untouched

Rome doesn't repent. It rebrands.

THE FRUIT **of a Rotten Tree**

> *"Every tree that doesn't produce good fruit is cut down*
> *and thrown into the fire." (Matthew 7:19).*

JESUS WARNED that bad fruit reveals a bad root. The papacy doesn't reflect Christ—it defies Him.

Yes, the Church feeds the poor. Yes, it builds hospitals. But so do the United Nations and Freemasons.

Good works don't sanctify spiritual rebellion.

CONCLUSION: Come out of Her

ASK YOURSELF: Would Jesus call these men "Holy Father"? Would He hand His Bride to murderers and occultists? Would He declare infallible those who burned His Word and butchered His followers?

The answer is obvious.

Critics argue that the historical papacy reflects political and moral corruption incompatible with Christ's model of shepherd leadership.

And Jesus is still calling:

> *"Come out of her, My people, so that you will not share*
> *in her sins." (Revelation 18:4).*

Sidebar — The House Is on Fire: A Catholic's Own Witness Against Rome

Some Catholics admit the Church has been infiltrated. Taylor Marshall, in his widely read book *Infiltration: The Plot to Destroy the Church from Within*, argues that Freemasons, globalists, and satanic forces didn't try to destroy the Catholic Church from the outside.

They wanted to possess it.

"The secret societies of Europe, particularly the Freemasons, were hell-bent on penetrating and corrupting the Catholic Church from within. They weren't trying to destroy the Church from the outside. They wanted to sit on Peter's Chair."[8]

He cites a 19th-century Masonic strategy known as the *Alta Vendita*, which outlined their plan to install a pope who would forward their agenda:

"We must have a Pope according to our needs... With that, we shall march more securely toward the assault on the Church than with the pamphlets of our brethren in France and the gold of England."[9]

Even Pope Leo XIII warned in his 1884 encyclical *Humanum Genus* that Freemasonry was no mere political nuisance—but a spiritual war against Christendom:

"A satanic sect bent on overturning the entire order of Christendom."[10]

And in modern times, Archbishop Carlo Maria Viganò confirmed that a Deep Church now mirrors the Deep State—one corrupted from within:

"The deep state is mirrored by a deep Church, filled with traitors who no longer serve Christ but serve globalist and Luciferian agendas."[11]

So what's the Catholic defense?

That the Church is "wounded but divine"?

That she's a "perfect bride" with a few unfaithful bishops?

That if we just clean house, she can be saved?

To that we say:

"Yes, the house is on fire — but if we kick out the arsonists, we can save the cathedral."

But his call to "save the Church" is like trying to clean the inside of the Titanic while it's sinking.

If even Taylor Marshall admits the Vatican has been infiltrated by Freemasons, globalists, and Luciferian agents, then what exactly are Catholics defending?

You don't patch up a corpse.

You bury it.

Or better yet — you walk out of the tomb.

Notes

1. Peter de Rosa, *Vicars of Christ: The Dark Side of the Papacy* (New York: Crown Publishing Group, 1988), 40–42.

2. de Rosa, *Vicars of Christ*, 45.

3. Philip Schaff, *History of the Christian Church*, vol. 5 (Grand Rapids, MI: Eerdmans, 1910), 322–324.

4. Avro Manhattan, *The Vatican Billions* (Ontario, CA: Chick Publications, 1983), 155–157. (Quote attributed; authenticity debated.)

5. de Rosa, *Vicars of Christ*, 33–38.

6. Pope Paul VI, Homily for the Solemnity of Saints Peter and Paul, June 29, 1972, Vatican.va.

7. Dave Hunt, *A Woman Rides the Beast* (Eugene, OR: Harvest House Publishers, 1994), 153–158.

8. Taylor Marshall, *Infiltration: The Plot to Destroy the Church from Within* (Manchester, NH: Sophia Institute Press, 2019), 80.

9. *Permanent Instruction of the Alta Vendita*, cited in Marshall, *Infiltration*, 103.

10. Pope Leo XIII, *Humanum Genus*, April 20, 1884, Vatican.va.

11. Carlo Maria Viganò, "Open Letter to President Donald Trump," October 25, 2020.

13

THE SYSTEM IS CRUMBLING
WHY THE MODERN CHURCH MIRROS THE DECAY OF ROME

"They will hold to a form of godliness but deny its power. Avoid such people." (2 Timothy 3:5, CSB).

When a pilot charts a flight path, even a one-degree deviation can lead to missing the destination by hundreds of miles. The modern Church hasn't drifted one degree. It's entirely veered off course. What began as a Spirit-led movement has mutated into lifeless ritual, political compromise, and institutional decay.

Jesus warned, "Don't let anyone deceive you in any way. For that day will not come unless the rebellion comes first" (2 Thessalonians 2:3, CSB). We're living in that rebellion now.

THE RITUALIZATION of Christianity

Cathedral Basilica of Saints Peter and Paul: The barren pews and towering ritual architecture reflect the spiritual emptiness warned of in 2 Timothy 3:5—"holding to a form of godliness but denying its power." While breathtaking in design, such spaces often symbolize performance without presence—tradition without truth. See Appendix R for full citation.

What defines most churches today? Sunday services that feel like stage productions. Worship of buildings over organic gatherings. Hierarchies that mirror corporate structures.

None of these resembles the early Church. Instead, they mirror:

- Pagan temple systems
- Catholic clericalism
- Protestant mimicry of Rome

The result? Dead religion, cloaked in Christian language.

THE EMPY-PULPIT CRISIS

THE SPIRITUAL FRUIT of this system is rotten:

- Studies from Lifeway and Barna consistently report high levels of pastoral stress, burnout, and depression.[1]
- 1,500 clergy leave the ministry every month.[2]
- Only 1 in 10 pastors retire while still in ministry.[3]

Meanwhile, Millennials and Gen Z are leaving in droves, while the "Nones" (no religious affiliation) are now the fastest-growing group in the West.[4]

Empty pulpits. Empty pews. Empty faith.

The great falling away isn't coming. It's already here.

SEMINARIES HAVE **Sold Out**

THE COLLAPSE BEGINS UPSTREAM.

Today's seminaries resemble Greek academies more than Spirit-filled upper rooms. They produce:

- Philosophers instead of prophets
- Professionals instead of pastors
- Politicians instead of disciples

Graduates often enter ministry without a fear of God, a working knowledge of the Holy Spirit, or a true understanding of the gospel. Many even question the inerrancy of Scripture before reaching their first pulpit.

Ed Kurath says, "Greek education produces religious flesh—people who speak about God without ever having met Him."[5]

THE DEMONIC RETURN **of the Priesthood**

. . .

"There is one mediator between God and mankind, the
man Christ Jesus." (1 Timothy 2:5, CSB).

THE NEW TESTAMENT abolished the priesthood. But religious
systems have rebuilt it—brick by brick:

- Protestant CEOs replaced Catholic bishops
- Celebrity pastors replaced humble servants
- Titles replaced testimonies

The biblical priesthood of all believers has been replaced by
an elite clerical caste that:

- Suppresses Spirit-led life
- Reinforces spiritual passivity
- Rebuilds walls Christ already tore down

This isn't biblical. It's demonic.

SEXUAL SCANDALS: Not Just a Catholic Problem

YES, the Vatican is infamous for abuse coverups. But Protestantism
is also guilty of:

- Pastoral sex abuse
- Victim suppression
- Denominational coverups
- Celebrity pastors falling into disgrace

The Spirit warned us, "Some will depart from the faith, paying attention to deceitful spirits and teachings of demons" (1 Timothy 4:1– 2, CSB). When churches reject the Holy Spirit, they reject God. Corruption fills the vacuum.

THE COLLAPSE of Western Christianity

EUROPE'S CATHEDRALS are now mosques, bars, and museums. Thousands of churches close every year in the USA.[6] "Christian" nations are post-Christian in both spirit and statistics.

> *"Because lawlessness will multiply, the love of many*
> *will grow cold." (Matthew 24:12, CSB).*

This lawlessness isn't cultural. It's spiritual—a rejection of God's presence in favor of human control.

THE RISE of the Religious Machine

MARKETING PLANS HAVE REPLACED PRAYER. Budget meetings have replaced deliverance. Sermons are designed to retain crowds—not rebuke sin.

Many churches today are well-lit tombs with fog machines. The Holy Spirit has left the building—and no one noticed. They are Laodicea in real-time:

> *"You say, 'I am rich,' but you are poor, blind, and*
> *naked." (Revelation 3:17).*

. . .

The Exodus Is Real—and **Righteous**

MILLIONS ARE WALKING AWAY from the modern Church. But not from Christ.

They're leaving:

- Programs
- Politics
- Performances
- Pulpit personalities

They're not rebellious. They're disillusioned. Many are obeying a divine call:

> *"Come out of her, My people, so that you do not share in her sins." (Revelation 18:4).*

The Voice **of the Remnant**

THE MOST ANOINTED voices today aren't in pulpits. They're in house churches, wilderness seasons, and YouTube corners. They speak with fire. They carry oil. They refuse compromise.

They don't have seminary degrees—but they have scars.

And that's enough for God.

A house church in China gathers for worship: Echoing the simplicity, intimacy, and Spirit-led focus of the early Church. Far from cathedral walls and clerical systems, these believers reflect what Jesus promised: "Where two or three are gathered in My name, I am there among them." See Appendix R for full citation.

Conclusion: Choose the Narrow Path

THE COLLAPSE of institutional Christianity isn't a tragedy. It's a prophetic fulfillment:

> *"Not everyone who says to Me, 'Lord, Lord,' will enter the kingdom of heaven." (Matthew 7:21, CSB).*

You must make decisions.

Will you follow the system or the Spirit?

Will you serve hollow religion or the living Christ?

Will you walk the wide road or the narrow path?

The true remnant will not be found in cathedrals, denominations, or megachurches.

They'll be found where two or three gather in Jesus' name—led by His Spirit, not man's traditions.

Notes

1. Lifeway Research, "Pastors' Mental Health and Burnout," 2021, https://lifewayresearch.com.

2. Lifeway Research, "1,500 Pastors Leave Ministry Each Month," cited in Thom Rainer, "Why Pastors Leave Ministry," 2019.

3. Barna Group, *The State of Pastors* (Ventura, CA: Barna Group, 2017).

4. Pew Research Center, "In U.S., Decline of Christianity Continues at Rapid Pace," October 17, 2019, https://www.pewresearch.org.

5. Ed Kurath, *Transformation New Testament* (Post Falls, ID: Divinely Designed, 2021), introduction and commentary sections.

6. Lifeway Research, "Church Closures Outpace Openings for the First Time," May 2021.

14

THE GREAT FALLING AWAY

HOW APOSTASTY AND ECUMENISM
SET THE STAGE FOR THE ANTICHRIST

"Let no one deceive you by any means; for that Day will
not come unless the falling away comes first, and the
man of sin is revealed." (2 Thessalonians 2:3, NKJV).

Before the return of Christ, Paul warned of a global deception —a falling away from the truth. Not just secular rebellion.

Not just persecution. A spiritual defection from within the Church.

The Greek word *apostasia* implies more than a gradual drift. It means a deliberate departure—a conscious exchange of truth for deception.[1] Many critics identify the medieval papal system as a primary historical example of such apostasy.

THE SEED of Apostasy

. . .

PAUL SAID the mystery of lawlessness was already at work in his day (2 Thessalonians 2:7). Even before the first century closed, false teachers were:

- Preaching another gospel
- Elevating man-made tradition
- Seeking power and prestige in the name of Christ

The early Church was barely born—and the enemy was already sowing tares among the wheat. The seeds of apostasy were planted early. Rome gave them a throne.

ROME: **The Engine of Deception**

Ponte Sant'Angelo: Spanning the Tiber with St. Peter's Basilica visible in the background at dusk. It is symbolic of how the rise of Rome and its rituals now bridge the spiritual gap from biblical truth to apostasy. See Appendix R for full citation.

The Catholic Church didn't merely fall away. It led the exodus from the truth. What was once biblical Christianity became Roman Catholicism.

Salvation by faith became salvation through sacraments.

Christ, as Head, became the pope as Vicar.

Scripture as final authority became tradition and Magisterium.

The priesthood of all believers became a clerical caste.

And one perfect sacrifice became a daily re-sacrifice in the Mass.[2]

This wasn't a reformation. It was a hostile takeover of Christianity.

Modern Christianity: Still Falling

However, Rome's influence didn't end at the Reformation. Today, many Protestant denominations are:

- Returning to Rome through ecumenical councils
- Embracing Catholic liturgy and feast days
- Promoting interfaith unity over biblical doctrine

In 2016, leading Protestant and Catholic leaders gathered in joint commemorations of the Reformation, reflecting a growing ecumenical convergence.[3]

The Rise of a Counterfeit Bride

While the true Bride of Christ prepares herself in holiness, a counterfeit bride is rising—draped in religion, powered by politics, and adored by the masses.

> "She had a golden cup in her hand full of abominations . . . and on her forehead a name was written: MYSTERY, BABYLON THE GREAT." (Revelation 17:4–5).

This counterfeit system will:

- Perform signs and wonders
- Preach tolerance and unity
- Silence biblical truth
- Persecute the true Church

It's not just misguided. It's the platform for the final deception.

KURATH'S WARNING: The Religious Spirit

ED KURATH DESCRIBES the religious spirit as Satan's most effective counterfeit:

"The religious spirit offers form without transformation, ritual without repentance, and control instead of surrender."[4]

It's a gospel that keeps people near Jesus—but not in Him.

Rome has perfected this system. And now, many Protestant churches imitate it.

THE ROLE of the Antichrist

PAUL WARNED that the great falling away would precede the revealing of the man of sin—the Antichrist.

The world is being primed by:

- Global interfaith agreements
- Ecumenical councils hosted in Rome
- A hunger for peace over truth

And at the center sits a religious figure who claims to speak for God on Earth:

> *"He will exalt himself above every so-called god . . . and sit in the temple of God, proclaiming himself to be God." (2 Thessalonians 2:4).*

This isn't speculation. It's Scripture—unfolding in real-time.

THE CALL TO **Remain Faithful**

JESUS WARNED that even the elect could be deceived—if possible. The only protection is truth.

Not tradition.

Not church affiliation.

Not an emotional experience.

But truth rooted in the Word of God—and in the living Christ.

CONCLUSION: **Come Out Before It's Too Late**

THE GREAT FALLING AWAY ISN'T a cultural trend. It's a prophetic fulfillment. It looks holy. It sounds spiritual. It feels safe. But it's the wide road that leads to destruction.

> *"Come out of her, My people, lest you share in her sins and receive her plagues." (Revelation 18:4).*

The system is falling. The Bride is rising. Don't follow the crowd.

Follow the Shepherd.

Notes

1. Frederick William Danker, ed., *A Greek-English Lexicon of the New Testament and Other Early Christian Literature*, 3rd ed. (Chicago: University of Chicago Press, 2000), 120.

2. Catechism of the Catholic Church, 2nd ed. (Vatican City: Libreria Editrice Vaticana, 1997), §1367.

3. Lutheran–Roman Catholic Commission on Unity, *From Conflict to Communion* (2013), Vatican.va.

4. Ed Kurath, *I Will Give You Rest* (Post Falls, ID: Divinely Designed, 2003), chap. 5.

15

SECRETS BREED WICKEDNESS (SPIRITUAL WARFARE EXPOSÉ)
VATICAN ARCHIVES, JESUIT AGENDAS, AND THE SPIRIT OF DECEPTION

"For nothing is hidden that will not be revealed, and
nothing concealed that will not be brought to light."
(Luke 8:17, CSB).

E vil thrives in the dark. That's why the most powerful institutions on earth rely on secrecy—especially when their mission is spiritual corruption cloaked in righteousness.

The Roman Catholic Church has perfected the art of concealment. It has hidden

- Doctrines
- Abuse
- Archives
- Alliances

And it's not just a historical footnote. It's happening now—behind Vatican walls, beneath papal robes, and inside "Christian" institutions around the world. Where there are secrets, there is wickedness.

The Vatican's **Love of Secrecy**

Few organizations have more classified material than the Vatican. Its Secret Archives (rebranded "Apostolic Archives" in 2019) contain over 53 miles of shelving, documents spanning more than 12 centuries, and restricted access to nearly all clergy and laypersons alike.[1]

Interior Storage, Vatican Apostolic Archive: Interior view of secured storage areas within the Vatican Apostolic Archive, showing controlled shelving and restricted archival access. The Vatican maintains one of the largest collections of historical religious documents in the world, many of which remain accessible only to approved scholars under strict conditions. The image illustrates how institutional authority has historically been reinforced through controlled access to information rather than open disclosure. See Appendix R for citation.

The archives allegedly house

- Papal correspondence with dictators
- Inquisition torture records
- Suppressed heresies and banned books
- Lost gospels and apocrypha

- Accounts of Marian apparitions and esoteric visions

A page from the 4th-century Codex Vaticanus B: One of the oldest and most complete Greek manuscripts of the Bible. Preserved deep within the Vatican Library for centuries, this text exemplifies Rome's role not merely as a guardian of Scripture but also as a gatekeeper to its access. While scholars can apply for access under strict criteria, critics argue that restricted access reinforces institutional control over historical narrative. See Appendix R for full citation.

Why hide these? Because truth threatens power. And Rome is built on controlling both.

Vatican Complicity in Global Crimes

In *The Vatican's Holocaust*, Avro Manhattan documents how the Church protected Nazi war criminals via the Ratlines, helped fund fascist death squads, and supported genocide against Orthodox Christians in Yugoslavia.[2]

This isn't ancient history. It's twentieth-century bloodshed under the banner of the cross. And to this day, the Vatican has never publicly repented.

The Jesuit Agenda

No religious order is more politically connected, intellectually respected—and spiritually dangerous—than the Society of Jesus.

Their original oath included the words, "I will ... extirpate and exterminate heretical Protestant doctrines . . . without pity or mercy."[3]

And while most modern Jesuits wear academic robes, not armor, their mission remains to infiltrate education, shape global policy, guide interfaith alliances, and subvert Protestant truth.

Sidebar: Jesuit Infiltration of Modern Institutions

- **Education:** Jesuit universities such as Georgetown, Fordham, Loyola, and Boston College teach a Catholic-flavored form of progressivism disguised as humanitarianism.
- **Politics:** Six of nine current U.S. Supreme Court Justices were raised Catholic; multiple presidents and advisers were trained at Jesuit institutions.
- **Media & NGOs:** Jesuit influence pervades the UN, Council on Foreign Relations, and even major tech ethics boards.

Jesuits rarely march in uniform anymore. They embed in systems —guiding from within.

. . .

ABUSIVE COVERUPS: **Global and Systemic**

TENS OF THOUSANDS of abuse cases have surfaced worldwide. Entire dioceses have been bankrupted. Vatican officials have repeatedly shuffled predators between parishes.[4]

This isn't just "bad leadership." It's organized, systemic evil—shielded by the institution itself.

Even Protestant megachurches mirror the same rot: celebrity pastors protected by PR teams, victims silenced "for the good of the Church," and repentance replaced by damage control.

THE BLACK ARCHIVES: **What's Still Hidden?**

SPECULATIVE CLAIMS MADE by certain researchers about a deeper level of Vatican secrecy:

- Unpublished prophetic scrolls
- Ancient pre-flood technology
- Babylonian magical rites
- Encrypted ET contact reports from the Vatican Observatory and the LUCIFER telescope[5]

Horn and Putnam write, "The Vatican holds secrets that, if exposed, would shake the foundation of global religion."[6]

For critics, such secrecy reflects not merely institutional caution but a deeper spiritual struggle over truth and authority.

Archival Document Analysis: An archivist examining historical manuscripts, representing the controlled handling and restricted access often surrounding religious and institutional records. The image illustrates how authority over history is maintained through selective preservation and interpretation rather than open transparency. See Appendix R for citation.

Jesus Was Never Secretive

JESUS DECLARED, "I have spoken openly to the world . . . I have said nothing in secret" (John 18:20). The true gospel

- Doesn't need walls
- Doesn't require guards
- Isn't encrypted

It's open, free, and dangerous to darkness. So, what kind of "church" builds vaults instead of altars?

THE SPIRIT of Deception

. . .

SECRECY IS the language of Satan:

> *"The thief comes only to steal, kill, and destroy"* *(John 10:10).*

Where you see secret doctrines, concealed abuse, censored dissent, and disguised agendas, you're seeing the fingerprints of the thief—not the Shepherd.

THE FINAL EXPOSURE Is Coming

JESUS PROMISED, "There is nothing covered that will not be uncovered, nothing hidden that will not be made known" (Luke 12:2, CSB). Rome can rewrite history, leaders can lie, files can be locked— but God sees all of it. And He's getting ready to judge.

CONCLUSION: Tear the Veil—and Step into the Light

THE GOSPEL ISN'T SECRET. The truth isn't buried. And the way out has never been easier to find.

Jesus tore the veil. The Spirit exposes the lie. And your freedom begins with one step:

> *"Come out of her, My people"* *(Revelation 18:4).*

You cannot break free from deception while living inside its fortress.

You must leave the shadows to walk in the Light.

Sidebar — The House Is on Fire, and They're Rearranging the Furniture

Even the most loyal Catholics, like Taylor Marshall, have publicly admitted the Catholic Church has been infiltrated by Freemasons, globalists, and Luciferian operatives. And yet—they still cling to the hope that the institution can be saved.

"Yes, the house is on fire — but if we kick out the arsonists, we can save the cathedral."

But his call to "save the Church" is like trying to clean the inside of the Titanic while it's sinking.

If even Taylor Marshall admits the Vatican has been infiltrated by Freemasons, globalists, and Luciferian agents, then what exactly are Catholics defending?

You don't patch up a corpse.

You bury it.

Or better yet — you walk out of the tomb.

Notes

1. Vatican Apostolic Archive, "Rescript of the Holy Father Francis," October 28, 2019, Vatican.va.

2. Avro Manhattan, *The Vatican's Holocaust* (Chino, CA: Chick Publications, 1986), chaps. 4–6.

3. Edmond Paris, *The Secret History of the Jesuits* (Chino, CA: Chick Publications, 1975), 41–49. (Note: The Jesuit oath has been contested by Catholic historians.)

4. Jason Berry and Gerald Renner, *Vows of Silence: The Abuse of Power in the Papacy of John Paul II* (New York: Free Press, 2004).

5. Thomas Horn and Cris Putnam, *Exo-Vaticana: Petrus Romanus, Project L.U.C.I.F.E.R., adn the Vatican's Astonishing Plan for the Arrival of an Alien Savior.* (Crane, MO: Defender Publishing, 2013), chaps. 2–4.

6. Ibid., 42.

16

HOW TO BREAK FREE FROM THE ROMAN CATHOLIC CURSE (LIBERATION GUIDE)

A STEP-BY-STEP GUIDE TO FREEDOM, DISCERNMENT, AND TRANSFORMATION

"You will know the truth, and the truth will set you free." (John 8:32, CSB).

Some readers might have already left the Roman Catholic Church physically, but spiritually, they still carry chains.

It may show up as confusion when reading the Bible. Persistent condemnation or fear. Dryness in worship. An invisible heaviness. An inability to move forward in intimacy with Jesus.

These are not just emotional leftovers. Many former Catholics describe lingering theological confusion or fear rooted in prior religious conditioning. This chapter addresses those spiritual and psychological patterns through biblical clarity and repentance.

THE CURSE IS **Real**

.   .   .

LET'S BE CLEAR: leaving the Catholic Church isn't the same as being free from it. The system is more than a theological error— it's a spiritual structure tied to:

- False covenants
- Blasphemous rituals
- Occult priesthoods
- Idolatrous oaths and images
- Bloodless sacrifices that deny Christ's finished work

When salvation is tied to sacraments, priestly mediation, and ritual repetition, believers can internalize a system of fear, obligation, and performance. Many believers walk away from the institution but never break the legal agreements they unknowingly made —agreements with false mediators, doctrines of demons, and ancestral idolatry.

What's a Curse?

A CURSE IS a spiritual legal structure rooted in rebellion, idolatry, or deception. It can be:

- Personal (resulting from personal participation)
- Generational (inherited through family lines)
- Institutional (entering into a covenant with a false system)

    "Cursed is anyone who makes a carved idol... and sets it up in secret." (Deuteronomy 27:15).

*"You cannot drink the cup of the Lord and the cup of
demons." (1 Corinthians 10:21).*

Catholicism, with all its beauty and form, is filled with what
God calls detestable things (Ezekiel 8–9). The curse continues
until it's broken.

LINGERING Effects of Religious Conditioning

EVEN AFTER BEING BORN AGAIN, many former Catholics struggle
with:

- Fear of condemnation
- Scrupulosity (obsessive guilt)
- Disconnection in prayer
- Lack of revelation from Scripture
- Passive submission to spiritual authority
- Unexplained shame or torment
- Anxiety over rituals or missing confession

These patterns are not accidental. They reflect years of forma-
tion within a system that places spiritual assurance in sacraments
and clerical mediation. When forgiveness feels conditional, and
grace feels earned, fear becomes the governing emotion of faith.

Psychologists have long documented a condition known as
scrupulosity—a religious form of obsessive-compulsive disorder
marked by excessive guilt, fear of divine punishment, and compulsive
confession.[1] Former Catholics are disproportionately familiar with
its symptoms, especially when salvation has been framed around

ritual performance and repeated absolution rather than finished redemption. While not every struggle is spiritual in nature, the psychological imprint of fear-based religion is real and measurable.

BIBLICAL FREEDOM REQUIRES Renunciation

THROUGHOUT SCRIPTURE, deliverance begins with separation:

- Abraham was called to leave his father's house.
- The Israelites had to forsake the gods of Egypt.
- The kings of Judah tore down high places.

Paul cast out spirits of divination and religiosity.

> *"Come out from among them and be separate... touch no unclean thing, and I will receive you." (2 Corinthians 6:17).*

The true gospel doesn't just forgive sins—it breaks yokes. And Jesus is still in the business of setting captives free.

HOW THE CURSE Gains Legal Ground

ACCORDING TO ED KURATH, the curse of Roman Catholicism takes hold through five doctrinal anchors that keep people bound:

1. **False Gospel** – Trusting sacraments, works, or Church membership over grace.

2. **False Mediators** – Prayers to Mary, saints, or popes instead of Christ alone.

3. **Occult Priesthood** – Belief in transubstantiation and the Eucharist sacrifice.

4. **Idolatry** – Veneration of images, relics, statues, and crucifixes.

5. **Covenants and Oaths** – Baptism into the Church, confirmation, Holy Orders, or marriage under its authority.[2]

Even if these things were done in ignorance, the spiritual realm recognizes them as legal claims—until they are broken in Jesus' name.

"My people are destroyed for lack of knowledge." (Hosea 4:6).

Chains are broken, freedom rises: This symbolic image represents deliverance from spiritual bondage—capturing the hope at the heart of your message: Christ sets captives free from manmade religion, deception, and control. See Appendix R for full citation.

Five Steps to Freedom: A Legal Act in the Spirit

THE CROSS NOT ONLY PAID FOR your sin—it annulled every false agreement made in your name.

*"He erased the certificate of debt... and has taken it
away by nailing it to the cross." (Colossians 2:14,
CSB).*

1. *Repent*

Acknowledge your participation in false religion. This
includes:

- Submitting to priestly authority
- Receiving the Eucharist as a repeated sacrifice
- Participating in Mass, confession, or rosary prayers
- Placing spiritual trust in Mary or saints

Ask God's forgiveness for putting anything above His Son.

2. *Renounce*

With your mouth, break every covenant made with Rome:
"I renounce every spiritual agreement I made with the Roman
Catholic Church—knowingly or unknowingly. I renounce every
false gospel, mediator, idol, and priesthood."
This isn't superstition. It's a legal act in the Spirit.

3. *Break Generational Ties*

If you come from a Catholic family:
"I break every generational curse and soul tie passed down
through my bloodline, in the name of Jesus."
Declare that Jesus—not your ancestry—is your source.

4. *Remove Objects of Bondage*

If certain objects reinforce misplaced trust, consider removing them from your spiritual life and replacing them with Scripture-centered practices.

- Statues of Mary or saints
- Rosaries, scapulars, medals, and holy water
- Catholic Bibles, missals, catechisms, or ritual candles

"Break down their altars, smash their sacred stones."
(Deuteronomy 12:3).

5. Release and Receive

Pray through the release prayers in Appendix B and Appendix C.

Take your time. Pray them out loud. Don't rush the Holy Spirit. Then receive:

- A fresh infilling of the Holy Spirit
- The truth of the gospel
- A clean conscience
- Freedom from fear

A WARNING AGAINST Religious Spirits

DELIVERANCE FROM CATHOLICISM isn't just doctrinal—it's spiritual. The religious spirit is one of Satan's most effective tools. It:

- Mimics holiness with external rituals

- Promotes effort over surrender
- Keeps people near Jesus—but not transformed by Him
- Replaces the voice of the Spirit with fear, guilt, and control

As Ed Kurath writes, "The religious spirit offers form without transformation, ritual without repentance, and control instead of surrender."[3]

Final Clarity: Breaking Free from Mistranslated Truth

Many who leave the Catholic system still carry its residue—not only in tradition but in how they read the Bible. That's because most English translations—especially those derived from Latin—have misrepresented key truths, leaving believers confused and bound. The following contradiction pairs are resolved in the Greek:

1 John 1:8 vs. 1 John 3:9

"If we say we have no sin..." vs. "Whoever is born of God does not sin."

Kurath explains the Greek emphasizes ongoing sin vs. the new nature's victory.

Colossians 2:13 vs. Matthew 6:14–15

· · ·

"HE FORGAVE ALL OF OUR SINS..." vs. "If you don't forgive, you won't be forgiven."

Kurath clarifies the distinction between relational fellowship and legal standing.

ROMANS 8:5 vs. Romans 7:15

"THOSE WHO LIVE ACCORDING to the flesh..." vs. "I do not do the good that I want."

Kurath shows Paul contrasts two inner laws, not Christian identity contradictions.

MATTHEW 6:13 vs. James 1:13

"LEAD US NOT INTO TEMPTATION..." vs. "God does not tempt anyone."

Kurath shows the Greek means deliverance, not divine temptation.

"What appear to be contradictions in English dissolve when you return to the Greek—revealing the clarity of God's Word."[4]

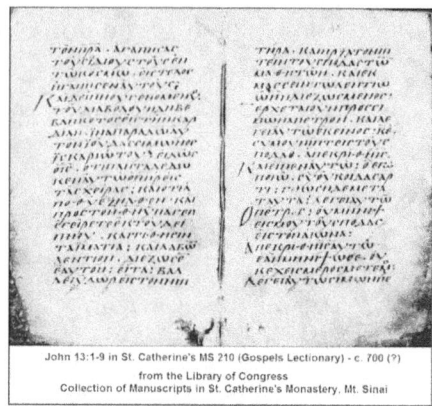

John 13:1-9 in St. Catherine's MS 210 (Gospels Lectionary) - c. 700 (?)
from the Library of Congress
Collection of Manuscripts in St. Catherine's Monastery, Mt. Sinai

*Greek manuscript fragment of John 13:1–9: Preserved in St.
Catherine's MS 210 (Gospels Lectionary), dating roughly to the
7th– 10th century. This sacred text, found at the foot of Mt. Sinai,
reminds us that spiritual truth flows from the direct words of Christ
—not from ecclesiastical dogma or human tradition. See Appendix
R for full citation.*

Ongoing Transformation: A New Way of Living

BREAKING free from the Roman Catholic system isn't a one-time
prayer. It's a call to a new way of life. You've renounced the counterfeit. Now, embrace the real. This means:

- Letting the Holy Spirit renew your mind (Romans 12:2)
- Learning the voice of your Shepherd (John 10:27)
- Living by grace—not guilt
- Worshiping without fear
- Walking in intimacy, not obligation

You don't need incense, candles, or rituals. You don't need
priests, popes, or catechisms. You have Jesus. You have His Word.
You have His Spirit. And that's enough.

. . .

Voices from the Wilderness

Throughout history, many saints have warned of religious deception. A few reminders:

- **Watchman Nee:** "The greatest hindrance to the life of Christ in a believer is the religious self."[5]
- **Leonard Ravenhill:** "God wants to raise up a people who are not seeking revival but seeking Him."[6]
- **A.W. Tozer:** "The essence of idolatry is the entertainment of thoughts about God that are unworthy of Him."[7]

These men all pointed to the same truth: God doesn't dwell in buildings made by man. He dwells in the yielded heart.

Conclusion: "Come Out of Her, My People"

This is your exit point. You don't need:

- Permission
- Priestly absolution
- Confirmation
- Deliverance ministry certification

You need Jesus. You need repentance. You need to renounce the lie and receive the truth:

"Come out of her, My people, so that you will not share

in her sins or receive any of her plagues." (Revelation 18:4).

Truth does not require permission. It requires courage. If Christ alone is sufficient, then no system can claim your conscience. Tear the contract. Close the door. Step out of Babylon —and into the freedom of Christ. He's waiting.

Now, turn to **Appendix B** to pray through your personal release. Then go to Appendix C, "A prayer Protestants should pray," to walk through the stronghold breakers in detail. And keep **Appendix A** nearby—it will help you read Scripture with fresh eyes.

Notes

1. Joseph W. Ciarrocchi, *The Doubting Disease: Help for Scrupulosity and Religious Compulsions* (Mahwah, NJ: Paulist Press, 1995).

2. Ed Kurath, *Transformation New Testament and Commentary*, rev. ed. (Self-published, 2021), Introduction and commentary notes.

3. Ibid., chap. 5.

4. Ed Kurath, "Key Verses" teaching notes (unpublished manuscript shared with author).

5. Watchman Nee, *The Normal Christian Life* (Wheaton, IL: Tyndale House, 1977), 104.

6. Leonard Ravenhill, *Why Revival Tarries* (Minneapolis: Bethany House, 2004).

7. A. W. Tozer, *The Knowledge of the Holy* (New York: Harper & Row, 1961), 11.

17

VOICES FROM THE EXIT DOOR (BONUS CHAPTER)
REAL TESTIMONIES OF ESCAPE

"You're not alone—and you're not crazy. You're just waking up."

(Anonymous ex-Catholic)

An open church door: Symbolizing quiet departures, unanswered questions, and the glimmer of light that beckons beyond religion and ritual. For many, the true journey of faith begins not at the altar, but at the threshold—when they walk away from man-made systems and toward Christ Himself. See Appendix R for full citation.

They don't advertise these stories. You won't hear them from the pulpit. You won't see them in a Vatican brochure. But behind the gilded icons and incense clouds are real people —millions of them—who've quietly walked away from the Roman Catholic Church and never looked back. Not because they hated God. But because their understanding of Him changed. These are their stories.

MARIA – Former Youth Minister, New York

"THE GUILT NEVER LEFT. I went to confession, said the rosaries, did penance. But I never felt clean. Not once."

Maria was raised Catholic from birth—baptized as an infant, confirmed as a teen, and later volunteered at her local parish for over a decade. But something always felt . . . off.

"Every time I sinned, I had to go back to the priest. But I kept asking—why did Jesus die if I still have to earn my forgiveness?"

After a failed marriage and years of spiritual exhaustion, she stumbled across a podcast teaching from the book of Romans. It forced her to reconsider everything she had been taught about grace.

"For the first time, I heard: 'There is now no condemnation for those in Christ Jesus.'1 And it didn't come from a collar. It came from the Word."

She now leads a home fellowship in her neighborhood, helping other Catholics make the transition out.

"I didn't leave Jesus—I left the structure I believed represented Him."

Most who leave do so quietly—no protest, no pulpit: Just a step into the light. This symbolic image captures the moment of personal exodus—when one walks away from religious control not in defiance, but in pursuit of truth, healing, and Christ Himself. The imagery visually reinforces the biblical call to leave systems of bondage and walk into revelation and freedom (cf. Revelation 18:4). See Appendix R for full citation.

David – Former Seminarian, Italy

"I WAS SUPPOSED to become a priest. My mother was thrilled. My grandmother cried tears of joy. But the closer I got to ordination, the less I saw Christ."

David studied at a prominent seminary in Rome. He knew Latin, theology, the Church fathers—and he knew how to keep secrets.

"There was a culture of silence," he says carefully. "Concerns were discouraged. Questions were redirected. Loyalty mattered more than transparency."

When a classmate came forward about abuse and was silenced, David began to question everything. He discovered Scripture on his own. He wrestled through Hebrews. He wept over Galatians.

"The Church said obedience. But the Bible said freedom. The Church said hierarchy. But Christ said, 'You are all brothers.' I had to choose."

David chose not to pursue ordination. He stepped away quietly and began reexamining the New Testament on his own terms. He now runs a small independent fellowship for ex-Catholics in southern Europe.

Some left with tears. Some left with nothing but a Bible: But all found something real on the other side. This moment captures the heartbreak of spiritual awakening—the quiet, personal rupture that precedes freedom. The cost is real. But so is the call. See Appendix R for full citation.

Teresa – Former Catholic School Teacher, Chicago

"I TAUGHT first graders to love the Eucharist. I taught second graders how to confess their sins to a priest. I was the good Catholic."

Teresa began noticing cracks after a former student was sexually abused by a trusted priest—and the bishop covered it up.

"They moved him to another parish as if nothing happened. I couldn't sleep. I couldn't teach the sacraments with a straight face."

Her personal crisis led to research, research led to Scripture, and Scripture led to Jesus—not the wafer, not the rosary—just Jesus.

"I had to unlearn everything. But once I met the real Jesus, I couldn't go back to a system that had come to replace the simplicity of Christ."

She now speaks at conferences for abuse survivors and advocates for the spiritual deprogramming of former Catholics.

Surveys by the Pew Research Center indicate that millions of Americans raised Catholic no longer identify with the Church.[1] Many describe their departure not as a rejection of faith, but as a search for clarity and authenticity.

FINAL REFLECTIN

THESE ARE JUST A FEW VOICES. There are millions more.

Some walked out quietly. Some left in protest. Some fled for their lives. But nearly all of them have one thing in common— they didn't abandon Christ. They abandoned the counterfeit.

"Come out of her, My people." (Revelation 18:4).

Notes

1. Pew Research Center, "In U.S., Decline of Christianity Continues at Rapid Pace," October 17, 2019.

POSTSCRIPT

May the eyes of precious Roman Catholics be opened, and may their hearts be stirred by truth.

May every soul who reads this book be drawn not to religion, but to Jesus Christ Himself.

❧

A Quick Note for Readers

If this book impacted you, please consider leaving a brief review at your preferred retailer. Even a few lines make a meaningful difference.

Thank you for reading carefully and thinking critically.

GLOSSARY
(DECODE THEIR LANGUAGE)

Quick Reference Sheet

Essential Terms for Understanding This Book

Anathema – A formal curse or excommunication declared by the Catholic Church against teachings or individuals deemed heretical.

Apostolic Succession – The Catholic belief that the Pope and bishops inherit their authority directly from the apostles through an unbroken line.

Catechism – An official summary of Catholic doctrine, used for teaching and reference by clergy and laity alike.

Ecumenism – The movement to promote unity among Christian denominations, often criticized in this book for diluting doctrine or leading to a one-world religion.

Eucharist (Mass) – The Catholic rite of Holy Communion. This book views the Mass's claim of re-sacrificing Christ as a denial of His finished work.

Idolatry – Worship of idols or created things. Often used in the book to describe veneration of saints, Mary, relics, and religious images.

Mariology – The Catholic theological study and veneration of Mary. This book sees it as unbiblical elevation of a human to divine-like status.

Papal Infallibility – The doctrine that the Pope cannot err when speaking "ex cathedra" on matters of faith and morals. Rejected in this book as an unbiblical claim.

Sacrament – Rituals believed by Catholics to confer grace (e.g., baptism, confirmation, Eucharist). This book critiques them as manmade additions to the gospel.

Sede Vacante / Sedevacantism – The belief that the papal seat is empty due to heresy by recent popes.

Syncretism – The blending of different religious systems. Often used in this book to describe the fusion of paganism with Christianity under Rome.

Tradition (Capital 'T') – In Catholicism, Tradition holds equal authority to Scripture. This book challenges that premise, upholding Scripture alone (sola scriptura).

Transubstantiation – The Catholic belief that bread and wine become the literal body and blood of Christ. Seen in this book as occult-like ritualism.

Veneration – The act of honoring saints, relics, or images. This book asserts it crosses into worship and violates biblical commands.

PART III

FOUNDATIONAL BREAKOUT

APPENDICES FOR DISCERNING BELIEVERS

For Further Study
Spiritual Tools, Historical Notes, and Freedom Prayers

The following appendices are offered for those who want to go deeper.

They include background research, historical evidence, freedom prayers, and renunciation tools rooted in Scripture.

This section is designed to support your continued journey out of religious bondage and into the freedom of Jesus Christ.

Read at your own pace. Revisit as needed. Use as a reference.

APPENDIX A

WHY CHRISTIANS NEED TO BE RELEASED FROM THE ROMAN PAGAN CURSES IMPOSED BY THE CATHOLIC CHURCH

Understanding Religious Entrenchment and Constantine's Fusion of Church and Empire

Everyone faces struggles—and Christians are no exception. Jesus came not just to forgive sin, but to transform us into His image. This process, known as *sanctification*, is part of salvation. Salvation has two aspects: a one-time event when we accept Jesus as Lord, and an ongoing journey of sanctification, cleansing, and being changed into His likeness.

When Christians feel spiritually stuck, sin is often the root cause. Sin produces "bad fruit" in our lives, and willpower alone can't fix it.

Our own sins open doors, which is why repentance and forgiveness are essential. Jesus forgives us—and we're called to forgive others (Matthew 6:14). Many Christians do this diligently, including forgiving those they've judged. Yet they often neglect to forgive themselves. And even then, some still feel stuck. At that point, something deeper may be at work—because Jesus *does* have the power to break every chain.

Pagan Influence Still Operates

Participation in non-Christian religious practices can create spiritual entrapment. If a believer has engaged in pagan rituals—even unknowingly—they must repent, renounce, and seek forgiveness. Most Christians recognize religions like witchcraft, Hinduism, or Buddhism as false. But they often overlook Catholicism—a paganized form of Christianity—and the Protestant denominations that inherited its traditions.

All Protestant churches are descendants of Roman Catholicism and still retain many rituals dating back to the time of Emperor Constantine.[1] These pagan elements have endured so long and become so normalized that their origins are often missed. But Satan hasn't missed them —and he exploits them to oppress believers.

The issue isn't just the *practice*—it's the *origin*.

If something originated from the Lord or Scripture, it carries divine authority. If it originated from Constantine's hybrid religion or pagan compromise, it can carry theological distortion or even demonic influence. For example, while believers gathered on the first day of the week in Acts 20:7, Constantine later institutionalized Sunday worship to align with *sun worship* customs of Rome.[2]

Idols are powerless on their own. But if your heart attributes obligation or holiness to something rooted in idolatry, it can open doors.[3]

The Spiritual Danger of Traditions

The New Testament doesn't just reinforce the Old Testament's warnings about idolatry—it sharpens them. Paul warns that "the sacrifices of pagans are offered to demons" (1 Corinthians 10:20). John pleads, "Keep yourselves from idols" (1 John 5:21). Idolatry is anything that competes for loyalty that belongs to God alone.

Here's the challenge: Do Catholics and Protestants believe Sunday is inherently holy—or is it merely a convenient gathering time? If that belief stems from tradition—especially one rooted in Constantine's decree—it could function as idolatry. If so, demonic influence may be operating through it. Only the Lord can reveal this.

If He shows you it's an idol in your heart, **repent**. Then ask if it's still acceptable for *you* to attend church on Sunday. Don't judge others— God sees their hearts.

Anything that replaces living intimacy with Jesus is an idol.

John writes in 1 John 5:20–21 that Christianity is a relationship, not a ritual system. Traditions are not inherently evil. But when they replace intimacy with control, they become spiritually dangerous.

Even if you didn't know a tradition was rooted in compromise, **sin is sin**—and hidden sin gives Satan legal ground. Jesus is eager to forgive, but He will not override your will. You must choose to see— and turn from—these patterns.

What If You've Embraced Pagan Traditions?

If you've embraced pagan customs as holy—even unknowingly— confess it, repent, and seek forgiveness. Without this step, Satan may continue exploiting open doors. He cannot operate without legal ground—and that ground is sin.

Jesus warned about spiritual vacancy: when a demon is cast out, but the heart remains empty, it can return with even greater oppression (Matthew 12:43–45). Forgiveness and sanctification *must* go hand in hand.

How to Break These Curses

1. **Work on your sanctification.**
2. This is your best protection against spiritual influence. Read *I Will Give You Rest* by Ed Kurath. As the Lord reveals what traditions are sinful in your life, repent.
3. **Pursue sanctification continually.**
4. If you stop growing, every new sin reopens old doors. Satan still *"roams about like a lion, seeking whom he may devour"* (1 Peter 5:8).
5. **Acknowledge the pagan origins of many Catholic and Protestant traditions.**
6. Many Christians respond well to prayer counseling. But when they don't, it's often because a *spiritual curse* is still active—often linked to Constantine's 325 A.D. fusion of paganism with Christianity.

These prayers do not attack any church. They acknowledge that even true believers can be spiritually afflicted by Rome's counterfeit system. Even with Christ's blood and the armor of God (Ephesians 6), cracks in the armor may exist. The Lord alone reveals them.

Protestantism Still Carries Rome's DNA

The Protestant Reformation exposed many Catholic errors, but it didn't break every link. Reformers like Luther and Calvin retained many Roman structures. Others—like Henry VIII—broke from Rome for political reasons, not spiritual ones.

Martin Luther never publicly renounced his priesthood, nor did he seek reconciliation with Rome. On the contrary, after Pope Leo X issued the 1520 bull *Exsurge Domine* demanding he recant, Luther publicly burned the document. At the Diet of Worms in 1521, he refused to retract his writings, declaring that his conscience was bound to Scripture rather than to papal authority. His later writings, including the *Smalcald Articles* (1537), hardened rather than softened his opposition to the papacy.[4]

That silence allowed many old frameworks to remain embedded in Protestantism.

Most modern denominations still carry remnants of what some call the **Constantine Curse**. But there is hope:

Through repentance, forgiveness, and the blood of Jesus, all curses can be broken.

Leftover "Traditions" Still Affecting Christians Today

Here are examples of traditions that **may serve as open doors**. Ask the Lord which, if any, affect you:

- Treating the Old and New Testaments as equally authoritative under the New Covenant
- Studying the Old Testament without recognizing the interpretive authority of the New
- Teaching that baptism washes away *all* sin permanently, eliminating the need for ongoing repentance
- Claiming all sins are automatically forgiven at salvation, even without confession or repentance
- Defining sin merely as "bad choices," minimizing its spiritual impact

- Teaching behavior and willpower are the keys to pleasing God, instead of Spirit-led surrender
- Emphasizing rule-keeping over love and relational obedience
- Teaching that God punishes believers when they're not "good," rather than seeing discipline as loving correction
- Celebrating Christ's resurrection through the modern holiday of **Easter**, which incorporates pagan symbols
- Treating the *doxology* in the Lord's Prayer as original Scripture, though it's not in the earliest manuscripts (Matthew 6:13)

Preparation for Prayer *(See Appendix B)*

Once you've identified traditions affecting you, bring them before the Lord.

The steps are:

- **Renounce** – to refuse to follow, obey, or recognize any longer
- **Repudiate** – to disown, break ties with, and fully reject
- **Repent** – to turn from sin and dedicate yourself to God's path

Forgive anyone who taught you these traditions. Then, in Jesus' name, command any demonic spirits to leave. Once the legal ground is gone, they have no right to remain.

Let the Lord fill you with His peace—and walk forward in freedom.

After each paragraph of the prayers in Appendix B, pause and ask the Lord if He has anything further to reveal about that area.

Notes

1. Dave Hunt, *A Woman Rides the Beast* (Eugene, OR: Harvest House, 1994), 233–235.

2. Constantine's civil decree regarding Sunday rest was issued on March 7, AD 321. See *Codex Justinianus* 3.12.2. For historical context, see Ramsay MacMullen, *Christianity and Paganism in the Fourth to Eighth Centuries* (New Haven: Yale University Press, 1997), 74–76.

3. Ed Kurath, *I Will Give You Rest* (self-published, 2003), chap. 6.

4. Roland H. Bainton, *Here I Stand: A Life of Martin Luther* (Nashville: Abingdon Press, 1950), 180–210; Martin Luther, *Smalcald Articles* (1537); Pope Leo X, *Exsurge Domine* (1520).

APPENDIX B

PRAYER OF RELEASE FOR ROMAN CATHOLICS AND THEIR DESCENDANTS

A Guided Prayer Framework (Adapted from Ed Kurath)

Note: These prayers draw on themes from Ed Kurath's *I Will Give You Rest.*[1] They are designed to help believers renounce false traditions, break spiritual bondage, and walk in freedom through the authority of Jesus Christ.[1]

This section uses terms like generational patterns, theological entrenchment, and spiritual conditioning. For definitions of these terms, consult the glossary and the notes on Constantine's religious fusion earlier in this book.

Father God, Creator of heaven and earth, I come to You in the name of Jesus Christ, Your Son. I come as a sinner, seeking forgiveness and cleansing from all my sins committed against You and others made in Your image. I honor my earthly father and mother and all of my ancestors—whether by blood, adoption, or spiritual connection—but I completely renounce all of their sins. I forgive all my ancestors for the effects of their iniquities on my life and the lives of my children. I desire to confess and renounce all of my own sins, accept the atoning sacrifice of Jesus Christ on the cross for me, and renounce Satan and every spiritual power of darkness affecting my family line in the name of Jesus.

Father God, I now understand that the Roman Catholic Church is not what it claimed to be. It is not a church dedicated to the Lord Jesus Christ but a deceptive religious system that masquerades as Christianity.

I acknowledge that I was deceived by its outward appearance. Though I recognized flaws, I did not see the full extent of its alignment with spiritual darkness. Had I known, I would not have participated in its practices or believed its teachings.

Even though I was misled, I take full responsibility for my own actions. Good intentions do not excuse my participation in spiritual error. Sin is still sin.

Father, although others played a role in my deception, it is ultimately my own sin that gave Satan legal access to influence me. But because of what Jesus has done, I can now be set free. Therefore, I renounce all evil practices and beliefs of the Roman Catholic Church, repent of my participation, and forgive others and myself. I ask You to forgive me. Cleanse me by the blood of Jesus, and release me from every demonic spirit that has gained access through these sins.

As I continue in this prayer, I ask You, Father God, to be present with me. Protect me, anoint these words, and guide me with any revelation I need.

I recognize that I came under a covenant of darkness when I became a Roman Catholic—either by my own choice or the decision of others made on my behalf. I reject and renounce every covenant made with the Roman Catholic Church, every agreement made with spiritual darkness, every refuge of lies, and every false covering.

I reject all ungodly involvement with Roman Catholicism by myself and my ancestors. I renounce every covenant, blood covenant, oath, or spiritual alliance ever made with the religious system or the spiritual forces behind it. I revoke all permissions—whether knowingly or unknowingly—granted to me or my family line. I repent for becoming entangled in this, and I ask You to break every chain and set me free.

Father God, in the name of Jesus Christ:

I reject every form of ungodly authority connected to the Roman Catholic hierarchy. I renounce false loyalty to the Pope and clergy when that loyalty should have been to Christ alone.

I renounce any impartation received through unbiblical laying on of hands or false priesthoods.

I renounce the doctrine of papal infallibility. Only You are true, and every man a liar (Romans 3:4).

I ask forgiveness for any honor I gave to people in religious offices or systems that denied Your truth.

I renounce the historical sins of the Roman Catholic Church—terror, bloodshed, torture, coercion, manipulation, immorality, and corruption. I forgive those who committed these acts and repent for any way I have aligned with them.

I repent for trusting a religious system that distorted and withheld the Word of God. I ask Your forgiveness for any way I altered, ignored, or resisted Your Word. Please renew my love for Scripture and teach me to apply it with clarity and conviction.

I reject the mixture of paganism and biblical teaching. I renounce every pagan belief and ask You to free me from all influence — mental, emotional, spiritual, or physical—that resulted from them.

I forgive those who taught me false doctrines, especially the lie of the "Sacrifice of the Mass." I reject calling on the spirits of the dead, which is forbidden in Scripture. I ask Your forgiveness for every way I participated in this deception.

I renounce all idolatry, including devotion to the "Holy Mother Church," and any form of spiritual adultery. I reject the veneration of Mary and all her false titles and roles. I acknowledge she was a humble woman who needed a Savior. I reject the doctrines of the Immaculate Conception, Perpetual Virginity, Bodily Assumption, and Co-Mediatrix teachings—none of which are found in Scripture. I ask Your forgiveness for participating in or believing these lies.

I reject all apparitions of Mary, including Fatima, Lourdes, Medjugorje, and others. I reject every message or instruction from these manifestations, as they contradict the Word of God. I reject all titles attributed to Mary that elevate her above what Scripture declares.

I renounce praying to the dead and the spiritism and necromancy involved in that practice. I forgive the Church for encouraging these things. I ask You to teach me how to pray in a way that honors You.

I cancel every dedication of my life to Mary or to any dead saint. I dedicate myself fully to the Lord Jesus Christ and to His purposes.

I renounce the false belief that saints can intercede for us. I reject every act of honor I gave to the dead that violated Your Word.

I renounce all trust placed in physical objects—medals, scapulars, statues, rosary beads, relics, votive candles, and more. I trusted in these things instead of trusting in You. I repent.

I renounce all unbiblical sacraments promoted by the Roman Catholic Church, including infant baptism, confirmation, Eucharist, confession, penance, and extreme unction. I ask forgiveness for my participation and recognize them as man-made rituals, not divine commands.

I renounce indulgences and the false teaching of Purgatory. I reject the idea that money or works can release souls from suffering or cancel sins. Lord, free my thinking from these deceptions and purify my heart in how I deal with money and salvation.

I renounce all ties between the Catholic Church and Freemasonry, the Mafia, the Jesuit Order, and any other occult, secretive, or antichrist organizations. I ask You to cut me off from all demonic influence that entered through these alliances.

I renounce every form of sexual immorality, perversion, and abuse associated with Roman Catholic clergy. I ask Your forgiveness for judging others or for any sin of my own related to this.

I renounce the unscriptural requirement of clerical celibacy, which has led to widespread abuse and dysfunction. I ask forgiveness for any role I've played in perpetuating or accepting this lie.

I repent of every sexual sin I have committed in thought, word, or deed. Father God, help me to resist temptation and walk in purity by the power of Your Spirit. Cleanse my heart and renew my mind.

I renounce legalistic fasting requirements imposed by the Church and all false guilt for violating them. I reject every death-dealing law not rooted in Scripture.

I renounce the teaching that infant baptism secures salvation. I affirm that salvation is a personal decision made in response to Your grace.

I now reject every remaining ungodly tie to Roman Catholicism— past, present, and generational. I revoke all permissions, pacts, or dedications made by me or on my behalf. I forgive those who led me into them. I ask You to break every remaining chain.

Lord Jesus, I thank You for Your forgiveness. Cleanse every

place in me that was defiled by these sins. Fill me with Your Spirit. Let no evil remain, and let no door remain open.

In the name of Jesus, I command every evil spirit that gained access through these sins to leave me now. You no longer have legal ground. You are evicted by the blood of the Lamb.

Curses: I declare that all curses are broken by the power of the cross. Jesus, You are my protector against every curse spoken by Roman Catholic entities or others.

Soul Ties: Father God, please sever every ungodly soul tie between me and any Roman Catholic or occult participant. Remove every spiritual residue and return to me what is mine, cleansed and restored.

Religious Spirits: I renounce every unclean spirit associated with Roman Catholicism, spiritism, and mysticism. I ask You, Father, to judge them and cast them to Your appointed place. Seal every portal through which they gained access.

Bondages: If any sin connected to the Roman Catholic system resulted in sickness, torment, addiction, emotional dysfunction, or spiritual bondage, I ask You to heal and free me completely.

Deception: Father God, I forgive those who taught me lies. I forgive Catholic leaders, followers, and even Christian leaders who failed to speak the truth. I release them all to You. Remove the veil of deception from my eyes and give me boldness and wisdom to speak truth in love.

Thank You, Father, for the ability to discern truth. Reveal any hidden falsehood I have yet to see. Give me clarity by Your Word.

I pray also for my family—those living and unborn. Have

mercy on my ancestors. Draw them to repentance. Break the generational curse. Set my descendants free to follow You in Spirit and truth.

Father God, if there is anything else I must repent of or pray through, please reveal it now. I yield to Your instruction. I trust You to fill every gap and cover every failure with Your mercy.

I thank You for hearing my prayer. I ask all of this in the name of the Lord Jesus Christ. Amen.

Pause to listen to God and respond as He leads.

Historical Reflection

This prayer framework is rooted in the conviction that spiritual transformation flows from repentance, forgiveness, and Scripture-centered faith. It is not a formula; it is a posture of yielding to Christ.

Many of the traditions renounced here have historical origins traceable to developments in early church history. For example, the civil integration of church and empire, beginning with Constantine's fourth-century reforms, reshaped many expressions of Christian practice.[2] The Protestant Reformation corrected many doctrinal errors but retained structural and ritual continuities from the medieval church.[3]

The heart of renewal is a return to Scripture — guided by the Spirit, not by external systems.

Notes

1. Ed Kurath, *I Will Give You Rest* (Post Falls, ID: Divinely Designed, 2003).

2. Ramsay MacMullen, *Christianity and Paganism in the Fourth to Eighth Centuries* (New Haven: Yale University

Press, 1997), discussing Constantine's influence on church structure and practice.

3. Roland H. Bainton, *Here I Stand: A Life of Martin Luther* (Nashville: Abingdon Press, 1950); Martin Luther, *Smalcald Articles* (1537); Pope Leo X, *Exsurge Domine* (1520), describing the persistence of medieval frameworks in the Reformation.

APPENDIX C

PROTESTANT PRAYER FOR RELEASE
FROM THE CONSTANTINE CURSE

Renouncing Spiritual Inheritance from Compromised Church Traditions

> *Note:* These prayers draw on themes from Ed Kurath's *I Will Give You Rest.*[1] They are designed to help believers renounce false traditions, break spiritual bondage, and walk in freedom through the authority of Jesus Christ. They are meant to lead believers into repentance and release from unbiblical traditions inherited through Protestantism's Roman roots.

Father God, Creator of heaven and earth, I come to You in the name of Jesus Christ, Your Son. I come as a sinner, seeking forgiveness and cleansing from all my sins committed against You and others made in Your image. I honor my earthly father and mother and all of my ancestors—by blood, adoption, or spiritual lineage — but I utterly renounce all their sins. I forgive my ancestors for the effects of their iniquities on my life and my children's lives. I now confess and renounce all of my own sins, and I receive the sacrifice of Jesus Christ on the cross for me. I renounce Satan and every spiritual power of his that has affected me or my family line, in the name of Jesus Christ.

Father, I now recognize that many Protestant churches, though dedicated to Christ in name, have inherited and embraced pagan traditions that originated with Constantine's corrupted church. I see now that these traditions have given place to the enemy and distorted Your truth.[2]

I also acknowledge that I was deceived. Though I knew there were flaws in Protestant churches, I didn't realize the depth of their compromise with pagan roots. I participated in spiritual error, believing lies, and engaging in practices that seemed biblical but were not. My good intentions do not excuse my sin. Sin is sin.

Even though others helped lead me into deception, it is my own sin that gave the enemy access. I can now be set free because Jesus died to cleanse me from all unrighteousness. So I now propose to reject and renounce all unbiblical practices and beliefs I embraced in Protestantism. I repent, forgive others, and forgive myself. I even forgive You, Father, for any way I blamed You. Wash me in the blood of Jesus, and free me from every demonic presence that gained access through these sins.

Be present with me now, Father. Anoint this prayer and protect this process. Speak to me and show me anything else that needs to be addressed.

Father God, I realize that by participating in Protestant traditions that originated in paganism, I came into alignment with a covenant of darkness—whether knowingly or through the actions of my parents or ancestors. I now reject and renounce every covenant, alliance, or permission made between myself (or my bloodline) and the spiritual forces behind those practices. I ask You to forgive me and break every chain.

I acknowledge that I was misled to think I was practicing true Christianity, but I now understand that some of those teachings and traditions were not from You. I forgive the Protestant establishment at every level for leading me into confusion and false worship. Forgive me, Lord, for believing and spreading these traditions.

You have revealed to me certain traditions that were not rooted in Your Word but in religious error. I now want to walk through those and be set free.

For each tradition the Lord has shown you:

- Recognize your participation in it as sin.
- Renounce and repudiate it.
- Repent and ask for forgiveness.
- Forgive those who led you into it.
- Ask the Lord to remove any bitterness or judgment and fill that area with His Spirit.

I also confess that I had never learned the importance of continual repentance and application of Jesus' blood for my daily sins. I now propose to walk in continual humility and confession, applying Your mercy daily.

In the name of Jesus Christ, I reject and renounce every other ungodly tie, covenant, alliance, and permission connected to Protestantism and the Constantine Curse. I forgive the Protestant churches that misled me. I repent, and I ask You to cleanse and restore me.

Thank You, Lord, for Your promise of forgiveness. Cleanse every dark place in me and fill each space with Your Holy Spirit. I know this is a miracle only You can perform. Thank You for Your mercy, love, and truth.

Because of the authority You've given me through Christ, I now speak directly to every spirit that gained legal access through these sins. I command you to leave me now in the name of Jesus Christ. You have no more legal right. These places are now filled with the Spirit of God.

Curses: Lord Jesus, I declare that every curse affecting me through these traditions is now broken. You are my covering and protection.

Soul ties: Creator God, please cut and dissolve every ungodly soul tie between me and any other Protestant or participant in false religion. Cleanse any intertwined part of my soul, and return to me what is mine, sanctified by the blood of Jesus. Seal all spiritual conduits with His blood.

Religious spirits: In the name of Jesus Christ, I renounce every religious spirit associated with Protestantism, spiritism, legalism, mysticism, or any counterfeit revelation. Pass judgment on them and send them to their appointed place.

Bondages: Father, if any sickness, emotional disorder, addiction, spiritual affliction, or bondage has resulted from these sins, I ask You now to release and heal me fully.

Deception: I forgive every spiritual leader who taught me error, knowingly or unknowingly. I forgive those who led others astray, and I ask You to show me how and when to speak truth to them in love. Open their eyes, Lord, and continue to reveal truth to me as well.

Help me distinguish between Your Word and manmade traditions. If I'm still deceived in any area, uncover it. Make Your truth clear.

I also intercede for my family—those living now and those yet to be born. Have mercy on them. Break off every generational curse and deception. Reveal Jesus to them in Spirit and in truth. Lead them out of error and into righteousness.

Father God, please show me if there's anything I still need to pray or do to complete this freedom. I trust You to lead me by Your Spirit.

I confess I am finite and fallible, but You are merciful and perfect. Cover anything I've missed and fill every gap. You know my heart. I offer this to You in humility.

I ask all of this in the name of the Lord Jesus Christ. Amen.

Pause and listen for the Lord's voice. Respond to anything He reveals.

Notes

1. Ed Kurath, *I Will Give You Rest* (Post Falls, ID: Divinely Designed, 2003).

2. Ramsay MacMullen, *Christianity and Paganism in the Fourth to Eighth Centuries* (New Haven: Yale University Press, 1997), 74–76; Dave Hunt, *A Woman Rides the Beast* (Eugene, OR: Harvest House, 1994); Alexander Hislop, *The Two Babylons* (Southampton, UK: Loizeaux Brothers, 1959); Ralph Woodrow, *Babylon Mystery Religion* (1990).

APPENDIX D
WHAT'S NEXT? WALKING FORWARD WITHOUT RELIGION

How to Live Free After Leaving a Religious System

> *"The ruler of this world is coming, but he has nothing in Me." (John 14:30, CSB).*

So, what happens now?

You've renounced religious deception. You've prayed to sever false covenants. You've begun to walk in spiritual freedom. But what about the practical side of your faith? What should you do next—especially if you've left a denomination or religious system?

This appendix offers guidance, not legalism. You're entering a new chapter—one of dependence on the Holy Spirit, not man-made rules.

You Don't Need to "Join" Another Church

Jesus never commanded you to join an institution. He called you to become part of His living Body.

That may look like:

- A small gathering in someone's living room
- A Spirit-led fellowship that rejects religious tradition
- Two or three believers praying together under a tree, in a home, or even online

What matters is not the structure—it's the presence of Christ:

> *"For where two or three are gathered in My name, I am there among them." (Matthew 18:20).*

Don't rush to replace your old church out of habit or loneliness. Let the Spirit plant you where truth and freedom can flourish.

Let the Holy Spirit Be Your Teacher

The Spirit of God is not silent. He is not vague. He will teach you —if you ask:

> *"But the Counselor, the Holy Spirit ... will teach you all things and remind you of everything I have told you." (John 14:26).*

Pray like this:

"Holy Spirit, lead me. I'm willing to be wrong. Show me where to go, what to study, and who to walk with."

Stay humble. Stay hungry. He honors both.
Be Patient with Yourself

You may still have questions like:

- "Is communion valid outside a formal church?"
- "What if my family still celebrates Catholic holidays?"
- "Can I read a Bible version printed by a denominational publisher?"

These are real concerns. And God isn't waiting to punish you for getting something wrong. Let the Spirit guide you into truth one layer at a time. Your spiritual detox may take weeks—or years. That's okay. He's not just freeing you. He's transforming you.

You're Still in the World—But Not of It

Even after deliverance, you'll still live in a world shaped by religious systems. You may find yourself:

- Working with people still in bondage
- Visiting churches that retain fragments of Rome
- Wrestling with traditions that carry emotional weight

Don't panic. You're not contaminated by proximity—only by participation.

Jesus walked among Pharisees, hypocrites, and idolaters. Yet He remained free—because none of them had any legal ground in Him:

> *"The ruler of this world is coming, but he has nothing in Me." (John 14:30).*

That's your new goal.

Final Word: Walk Boldly

This isn't about perfection. It's about purity of allegiance.

You belong to Christ—not to Rome, Constantine, or systems of religious control.

You've been released. Now, walk as one who is truly free.

The journey doesn't end here.

It begins here.

PART IV

DOCTRINAL DETOX

UNLEARNING RELIGIOUS LIES — REDISCOVERING GOD'S TRUTH

APPENDIX E

WHAT THE BIBLE SAYS ABOUT
CONFESSION VERSUS REPENTANCE

Debunking the Catholic Sacrament of Penance with Scripture

> *"If we confess our sins, He is faithful and righteous to forgive us our sins and to cleanse us from all unrighteousness." (1 John 1:9, CSB).*

The Roman Catholic Church teaches that confession to a priest is required for forgiveness. But the Bible tells a very different story—one of direct access to God through Jesus Christ alone.

Scripture never commands us to confess our sins to a human priest. Instead, the entire New Testament affirms that Jesus is our High Priest (Hebrews 4:14–16) and that forgiveness is granted through Him—not through ritual or institution.

The Biblical Model: Confession + Repentance = Forgiveness

True biblical confession is not a ritual. It is a relational act between the believer and God. It flows from a heart convicted by the Holy Spirit and a willingness to turn from sin.

- **Confession** means agreeing with God about your sin.
- **Repentance** means turning away from sin and turning back to God.

"Repent and believe the good news!" (Mark 1:15).

The Catholic sacrament of penance encourages confession to a man, followed by acts of contrition. But Jesus and the apostles never commanded confession to clergy.

Instead, the Bible gives us examples of direct confession and repentance:

- The tax collector who cried out, "God, have mercy on me, a sinner" (Luke 18:13)
- The thief on the cross, who was forgiven without a priest (Luke 23:40–43)
- Peter, who called for repentance at Pentecost with no mention of human mediators (Acts 2:38)

Jesus Never Said "Confess to a Man"

Catholic doctrine claims that priests act *in persona Christi*—in the person of Christ—during confession. But the Bible states:

"There is one God and one Mediator between God and mankind, the man Christ Jesus." (1 Timothy 2:5).

Confessionals, absolution, and priestly mediation were later inventions—not established by Jesus, the apostles, or the Holy Spirit.

The Early Church Never Practiced It

The book of Acts and early historical records show that the early Church:

- Encouraged mutual confession in the context of fellowship and prayer (James 5:16)
- Emphasized repentance and faith—not religious rituals
- Taught that conviction comes through the Holy Spirit, and forgiveness through Christ alone (John 16:8; Colossians 1:14)

In short, New Testament confession was:

- **Horizontal** (believers sharing in accountability)
- **Vertical** (between the believer and God)
- **Never hierarchical** (through clergy or religious authority)

Final Word: Confession Leads to Relationship, Not Ritual

Forgiveness is not accessed through sacraments. It's accessed through a Savior.

Jesus never said, "Confess to a priest." He said:

> *"Come to Me, all of you who are weary and burdened, and I will give you rest." (Matthew 11:28).*

Key Takeaways

- True confession—not a confessional booth—brings you to Christ.
- True repentance—not penance—produces fruit.
- True forgiveness is already paid for—not earned through ritual.

The goal is restoration, not ritual. Relationship, not religion. Christ, not clergy.

APPENDIX F
THE JEZEBEL SPIRIT IN RELIGIOUS SYSTEMS

How Control, Fear, and Clericalism Replace Christ's Authority

> *"You tolerate the woman Jezebel, who calls herself a*
> *prophetess and teaches and deceives My servants."*
> *(Revelation 2:20, CSB).*

The Jezebel spirit isn't only about sexual immorality. At its core, it's about religious control—manipulating worship, silencing truth, and hijacking spiritual authority within the Church. This spirit thrives in systems that exalt man, muzzle the Holy Spirit, and crush prophetic voices.

Jezebel doesn't always wear red. She sometimes wears a robe.

Where Jezebel Hides

The Jezebel spirit thrives in:

- Churches where leaders demand submission but never serve
- Movements that silence prophetic correction Systems that weaponize guilt, fear, and tradition to maintain power
- Environments where rituals replace relationship
- Hierarchies that exalt clergy and suppress discernment

This spirit operates across denominations. It is as comfortable in Catholicism as it is in charismatic networks. Jezebel doesn't care about your theology—she cares about power.

How It Works

Jezebel's methods are timeless:

- **Charisma** to seduce
- **Authority** to control
- **Flattery** to disarm
- **Fear** to silence opposition

It targets leaders, manipulates doctrine, and demands loyalty to the system—not to Christ. What may start as "honor for leadership" quickly becomes spiritual slavery.

What It Produces

When tolerated, the Jezebel spirit produces:

- Stagnant congregations
- Powerless worship
- Fear-based obedience

- Clerical elitism
- Burned-out pastors
- Silenced prophets
- Spiritually paralyzed believers

The Church becomes a stage for performance, not a temple of living stones.

How to Break Free

Stop tolerating it. Jezebel gains power through permission. Confront it spiritually:

- **Repent** of any participation in control—whether through submission to unbiblical authority or willful silence **Forgive** those who operated under it. Many are deceived themselves
- **Renounce** spiritual fear and religious idolatry. Break covenants that exalt man above Christ
- **Reclaim** your spiritual inheritance. You were called to freedom, not bondage

  "Where the Spirit of the Lord is, there is freedom." (2 Corinthians 3:17).

Final Word

You were not born again to serve a religious empire. You were redeemed to walk in Spirit and truth.

Jezebel still operates in churches that fear disruption more than deception. But Jesus said:

"I gave her time to repent . . . but she was unwilling."
(Revelation 2:21).

Don't tolerate it. Don't excuse it. **Expel it.**

APPENDIX G

ROMAN CATHOLIC SYMBOLS
AND THEIR PAGAN ORIGINS

Visual Proof of Idolatry and Syncretism Still in Use Today

> *"Do not learn the way of the nations . . . For the customs of the peoples are worthless." (Jeremiah 10:2–3, CSB).*

> *"They exchanged the truth of God for a lie, and worshiped and served what has been created instead of the Creator." (Romans 1:25).*

Many Catholic symbols—though wrapped in religious tradition—were never instituted by Christ or His apostles. Instead, they were borrowed from pagan cultures to ease Rome's transition into Christianity. But what is adopted from darkness remains spiritually dangerous, even when relabeled.

Why Symbols Matter

- Symbols carry spiritual weight, not just visual meaning.
- God warns explicitly against idolatrous objects:

"You shall not make for yourself an idol . . . You shall not bow down to them or serve them." (Exodus 20:4–5).

- The Church is not permitted to repurpose demonic imagery for "holy" use.
- What begins as "veneration" often becomes worship in disguise.

Common Catholic Symbols with Pagan Roots

The following are prominent symbols found throughout Catholic tradition, all of which trace back to ancient pagan practices:

- **Obelisks** — Ancient Egyptian sun worship; rebranded and placed in St. Peter's Square
- **Sunbursts / Monstrance** — Used in the worship of Ra and Mithras
- **Statues of Mary / Queen of Heaven** — Echoes of Semiramis, Isis, and Diana
- **Halos / Circular Auras** — Pagan solar disc iconography adopted in saint paintings
- **Pinecones** — Symbol of spiritual enlightenment in Babylon and Rome; now in Vatican Court
- **Keys of Peter** — Visually identical to symbols used by Janus, the pagan god of doorways
- **Vesica Piscis** — Feminine fertility symbol used in Marian art and cathedral windows

- **Crossed Keys and Triple Crown** — Papal regalia with striking similarity to symbols of authority used by Babylonian priests

God's Warning About Images

Catholic defenders argue these items are just "visual aids." But God doesn't differentiate based on intent when the result mirrors pagan idolatry. Lighting candles, kneeling before statues, and carrying relics in processions replicate ancient rituals God detested.

God sees no difference between intentional idolatry and ritual repetition rooted in deception.

What the Early Church Used Instead

The early Church kept worship free from visual idols:

- Spirit-led gatherings without icons
- No use of statues, incense, or relics
- Home-based worship and communion in simplicity

Their reverence was for Christ Himself—not an object or image. Christ was present by His Spirit, not confined to carved stone or metal.

Final Word

The Roman Catholic Church didn't reform paganism. It baptized it— and kept the idols.

Jesus does not need golden sunbursts, marble statues, or clouds of incense. He seeks hearts that worship in spirit and truth.

"Flee from idolatry." (1 Corinthians 10:14).

If the symbol leads to reverence, and the reverence leads to idolatry—then the symbol must go.

APPENDIX H

IDOLATRY AND THE SECOND COMMANDMENT

What the Bible Says About Statues, Relics, and Veneration

> *"You shall not make for yourself an idol . . . You shall not bow down to them or serve them." (Exodus 20:4–5, CSB).*

> *"They have mouths but cannot speak . . . those who make them will become like them." (Psalm 115:5–8).*

The Second Commandment is clear: Do not make carved images or bow down to them in worship. Yet in Roman Catholic catechisms, this commandment is conspicuously absent. To preserve a total of ten, the Church:

- Removed the Second Commandment against graven images
- Split the Tenth Commandment into two (coveting your neighbor's wife vs. possessions)

This is not a formatting error. It's a deliberate spiritual omission.

What Scripture Forbids

The Second Commandment specifically warns:

- Do not create idols
- Do not bow to them
- Do not serve them

These prohibitions apply to:

- Statues of saints and angels
- Marian shrines and images
- Crucifixes and sacred relics
- Venerated objects kissed, carried, or encased in gold

Catholic apologists may deny they "worship" statues—but their actions tell another story:

- Kneeling
- Lighting candles
- Touching garments
- Offering flowers
- Whispering prayers

> *"You shall not bow down to them or serve them."*
> *(Exodus 20:5).*

Intentions do not sanctify disobedience. Only submission to God's Word does.

Historical Tampering

- The Catholic Catechism omitted the Second Commandment as early as the ninth century
- Early Church Fathers warned against images—but were later ignored
- The Council of Trent (1545–1563) formally endorsed sacred images

The result? Cathedrals filled with relics, statues, and incense—mirroring pagan temples. This was not Christian restoration. It was Babylonian regression in religious disguise.

The Danger of Veneration

God doesn't ask for visual aids. He asks for undivided spiritual devotion.

Veneration leads to:

- Emotional attachment to objects
- Subconscious reliance on idols
- Confusion between Creator and creation

Statues may seem harmless—but when reverence transfers to the object, the altar becomes a trap.

Final Word

You do not need an image to worship Jesus. You need the Holy Spirit and truth.

If your faith depends on icons, relics, or rituals, you may not be worshiping the Christ of Scripture. The Second Commandment was not optional. It was carved in stone.

> *"God is spirit, and those who worship Him must worship*
> *in spirit and in truth." (John 4:24).*

Break the statues. Burn the relics. Return to the God who sees no form—only faith.

APPENDIX I

QUESTIONS EVERY CATHOLIC SHOULD ASK

Scripture-Based Challenges to Core Doctrines and Practices

> *"Test everything; hold fast to what is good."* (1 Thessalonians 5:21, CSB).

> *"My people are destroyed for lack of knowledge."* (Hosea 4:6).

Many Catholics are sincere in their devotion. They love tradition, revere authority, and assume the Church speaks for Christ. But sincerity doesn't equal truth. Jesus never asked for blind faith in religious systems—He called for truth that sets you free (John 8:32).

The questions below aren't intended to insult. They're meant to awaken.

Seven Questions Every Catholic Should Ask

1. Why is the Bible's Second Commandment missing from your catechism?

Exodus 20:4–5 forbids the worship of statues and bowing down to images. If God commands it, why did the Church remove it?
Why must I confess to a man instead of directly to God?

> *"If we confess our sins, He is faithful . . ."* (*1 John 1:9*).

> *"There is one Mediator . . . Christ Jesus."* (*1 Timothy 2:5*).

Jesus never said, "Tell your sins to a priest."

2. Why is salvation dependent on sacraments instead of faith alone?

> *"It is by grace you have been saved . . . not by works."* (*Ephesians 2:8–9*).

3. If grace is a gift, why must it be dispensed by clergy?

4. Why is Mary exalted as Queen of Heaven, Co-Redeemer, or Mediatrix?

> *"My spirit rejoices in God my Savior."* (*Luke 1:47*).

> God condemns the worship of the "*Queen of Heaven.*" (*Jeremiah 7:18*).

Mary pointed to Christ—not herself.

5. Why are popes called Holy Father, Vicar of Christ, or infallible?

> *"Call no man on earth your father." (Matthew 23:9).*

> *"Christ alone is Head of the Church." (Colossians 1:18).*

There is no biblical pope—only a risen King.

6. Why are traditions treated as equal to Scripture?

> *"You nullify the word of God by your tradition." (Mark 7:13).*

The Word of God doesn't need help. It needs obedience.

7. Why did the Catholic Church persecute those who translated the Bible?

> *"All Scripture is God-breathed." (2 Timothy 3:16).*

Wycliffe, Tyndale, and Luther were hunted—not for heresy, but for making God's Word available to the people.

Final Reflection

If your church can't answer these questions with Scripture alone, then you may be following tradition more than truth. Jesus said,

> *"You nullify the word of God by your tradition that you have handed down" (Mark 7:13).*

Ask the questions. Search the Scriptures. And let the Holy Spirit —not the Magisterium—lead you into all truth.

> "If you continue in My word, you really are My disciples. You will know the truth, and the truth will set you free." (John 8:31–32).

PART V

CHAINS AND LIES BROKEN

DELIVERANCE, EXPOSURE, AND FINAL FREEDOM

APPENDIX J
BREAKING GENERATIONAL RELIGIOUS STRONGHOLDS

How Spiritual Oppression Can Be Inherited—and How to Break Free

> *"Christ redeemed us from the curse of the law by becoming a curse for us." (Galatians 3:13).*

> *"You shall not bow down to them or serve them . . . visiting the iniquity of the fathers on the children to the third and fourth generation." (Exodus 20:5, ESV).*

Religious bondage doesn't always begin with you. If your parents, grandparents, or ancestors were immersed in fear-based religion, clerical control, false doctrine, or idolatrous traditions, you might have inherited a spiritual residue—even if you left the Church long ago. Many former Catholics discover that leaving an institution does not immediately untangle the theological patterns formed over years of participation. These generational strongholds are real. And unless they're recognized and renounced, they can subtly influence your:

- Beliefs about God
- View of authority
- Experience of the Holy Spirit
- Relationship with Scripture
- Ability to walk in freedom

What Are Generational Religious Strongholds?

A generational stronghold is a recurring spiritual pattern passed down through family lines. These patterns are often rooted in:

- False covenants made through religious rituals (infant baptism, confirmation, priesthood vows, and so on)
- Fear-based theology that exalts punishment over grace
- Idolatry (for example, Marian devotion, saint veneration, relics)
- Clerical submission to unbiblical spiritual authorities
- Religious trauma involving guilt, shame, or performance-driven faith

These strongholds can remain dormant—until you try to walk in freedom. Then, the spiritual resistance begins.

Common Symptoms of Inherited Religious Bondage

- Deep fear of God as an angry judge
- Shame, even after confessing sin
- Confusion while reading Scripture
- Feeling unworthy of grace or spiritual gifts

- Guilt over leaving the Church or breaking family tradition
- Hesitance to trust the Holy Spirit directly

If you've experienced any of these, the root may not just be psychological—it may be spiritual.

How to Break Religious Strongholds

> *"If the Son sets you free, you will be free indeed." (John 8:36).*

Deliverance is available—but it must be intentional. The following are steps toward breaking generational religious bondage:

- Acknowledge your family's religious background, and honestly repent for any personal agreement you've made with those systems
- Forgive those who passed it on—even if they meant well
- Renounce every false spiritual covenant (e.g., sacramental pledges, vows to religious orders)
- Command every religious spirit to leave in Jesus' name
- Replace the lies with Scripture and Spirit-led truth

Example Prayer Declaration

In the name of Jesus Christ, I break all generational strongholds inherited from religious systems that oppose the Word of God. I renounce every spiritual tie to false priesthoods, sacraments, idolatry, and man-made tradition. I cancel all agreements made on my behalf and release myself from every unbiblical authority. Holy Spirit, fill every place where bondage was—lead me into all truth. I'm free. I'm clean. I'm Christ's alone. Amen.

Final Word

Jesus didn't come to start a religion. He came to destroy the works of the Devil—including the ones passed down through families.

> *"You nullify the word of God by your tradition that you have handed down." (Mark 7:13).*

Break the cycle. Burn the bridge. Walk in the Spirit—and never go back.

APPENDIX K

THE SIMPLICITY OF THE GOSPEL

A Beautiful Reminder of What Religion Complicates—and What Christ Completed

"It is finished." (John 19:30).

"I am not ashamed of the gospel, because it is the power
of God for salvation to everyone who believes."
(Romans 1:16).

In the noise of religion, tradition, and theology, it's easy to lose sight of what truly saves. The gospel isn't a:

- Ritual
- Denomination
- Sacrament
- System

It's a person—Jesus Christ. And His gospel is stunningly simple.

What the Gospel Says

- You were dead in your sin.
- Christ died in your place.
- He rose from the dead.
- Anyone who believes in Him and continues faithfully to the end is saved.

> *"But the one who endures to the end will be saved."*
>   *(Matthew 24:13).*

> *"Now that you have been set free from sin and have become slaves of God, the fruit you get leads to sanctification and its end, eternal life." (Romans 6:22).*

> *"By this gospel you are saved, if you hold firmly to the word I preached to you." (1 Corinthians 15:2).*

No rosaries. No priestly absolution. No works-based ladders to heaven.

> *"By grace you have been saved through faith—and this is not from yourselves, it is the gift of God—not by works, so that no one can boast." (Ephesians 2:8–9).*

What It's Not

The gospel is not:

- "Start with Jesus, continue with sacraments."
- "You must go through Mary."
- "The Church dispenses grace."
- "Faith plus works equals salvation."

That's not good news. That's spiritual slavery.

The Gospel Frees You

It frees you from:

- Fear of not being good enough
- Guilt that never lifts
- Confession booths and man-made rituals
- Endless penance and religious obligations

What Jesus Said

> *"Come to Me, all of you who are weary and burdened, and I will give you rest." (Matthew 11:28).*

> *"The one who believes in Me will never thirst." (John 6:35).*

> *"No one comes to the Father except through Me." (John 14:6).*

Jesus didn't say, "Come to the Church." He said, "Come to Me."

Final Word

The gospel isn't complicated. It's clear. It's complete. And it's available —right now.

"It is finished." (John 19:30).

It's none of the following:

- "It began with the Church."
- "Continue it with sacraments."
- "Cling to tradition and hope you've done enough."

The gospel is *finished*. Christ is enough. No priest required. No mediator but Him. No system, no striving—only surrender.

∽

Believe. Receive. Be free.

APPENDIX L

THE FALSE PETRINE FOUNDATION

Why Peter Was Never a Pope—and Why It Matters

"Nothing mortal is so unstable and subject to change as power which has no foundation." — Tacitus

"For no one can lay any foundation other than what has been laid down. That foundation is Jesus Christ." (1 Corinthians 3:11, CSB).

The Roman Catholic Church claims an unbroken line of succession from the apostle Peter. It teaches that Peter was the first pope, appointed directly by Jesus, and that every pope since holds the keys to Christ's kingdom. But is this claim biblically or historically accurate?

If Peter was never appointed pope—and if no such office was ever instituted by Christ—then the doctrinal basis for papal supremacy stands on a false foundation. This isn't a minor doctrinal disagreement. It's a seismic fault line beneath the Vatican itself.

The Petrine Theory

The central Roman Catholic claim rests largely on one passage:

> *"And I also say to you that you are Peter, and on this*
> *rock I will build My church" (Matthew 16:18, NET).*

But a closer examination of the Greek text, historical context, and the rest of Scripture tells a different story.

- *Wordplay, not coronation:* Jesus uses two distinct Greek words: petros (a movable stone) and petra (a massive foundational rock). Jesus—not Peter—is the Rock (see 1 Corinthians 10:4; 1 Peter 2:6–8).[1]
- *No papal appointment in the New Testament:* The New Testament nowhere depicts Peter as a pope. He serves alongside others. At the Jerusalem Council (Acts 15), James —not Peter—renders the final decision.
- *Rebukes and failures:* Peter was publicly rebuked by Paul for hypocrisy and doctrinal error (Galatians 2:11–14). That would not be possible if Peter were infallible.

The Rise of the Roman Papacy

If the Bible doesn't support Peter as pope, then where did the idea come from? Answer: power, politics, and prestige—not Scripture. Historically, the development of a centralized episcopal authority in Rome appears gradual rather than immediate:

- By the second and third centuries, churches began appointing bishops. Rome's bishop gained influence due to the city's geography and tradition of martyrdom (Peter and Paul).[2]
- The Council of Nicaea (325 AD) didn't grant supremacy to the bishop of Rome.[3] It recognized him as only one of several major regional authorities.
- In 440 AD, Pope Leo I ("Leo the Great") declared papal supremacy, claiming that all church authority flowed from Peter's throne.[4]
- The title *Pontifex Maximus*—once held by Roman emperors—was later adopted by the popes, reinforcing a pagan title of divine rulership.[5]
- Ironically, Pope Gregory I (590–604 AD) rejected the title "universal pope," deeming it a precursor to the Antichrist.[6] Yet, centuries later, the Church that bears his name embraced the very claim he condemned.

The Dangerous Consequences of a False Foundation

If Rome's authority is built on Peter—and Peter was never pope—then the foundation is fatally flawed.

> *"Everyone who hears these words of Mine and doesn't act on them will be like a foolish man who built his house on the sand." (Matthew 7:26).*

A false foundation produces false fruit:

- Spiritual confusion: Salvation is redirected from Christ to sacraments and priesthood.

- False assurance: Rituals and rites replace personal relationship.
- Suppression of Scripture: Catholicism historically limited access to the Bible.
- Persecution of Reformers: Wycliffe, Tyndale, Luther, and Huss were silenced or executed for challenging papal claims.

Paul warned about human tradition displacing Christ's primacy:

> *"I'm afraid that just as Eve was deceived by the serpent's cunning, your minds may be led astray from pure devotion to Christ." (2 Corinthians 11:3).*

Conclusion: Christ Is the Rock

> *"For no one can lay any foundation other than the one already laid, which is Jesus Christ." (1 Corinthians 3:11).*

> *"The Lord is my rock, my fortress, and my deliverer." (Psalm 18:2).*

The true Church isn't built on Peter. It's built on Jesus, the Cornerstone (Ephesians 2:20). Any system that exalts a man to divine authority, claims infallibility, or places a throne in place of a cross is a counterfeit kingdom. Any structure that claims ultimate spiritual authority must be measured against Scripture and historical evidence.

The Call Is Clear

Come out of the deception.

Stand on the true Rock. Follow Christ alone.

Notes

1. Edward Kurath, *You Can Read the Greek: The Easy Way* (Golden, CO: Divinely Designed, 2015), 31–34.

2. Dave Hunt, *A Woman Rides the Beast* (Eugene, OR: Harvest House Publishers, 1994), 78–82.

3. William Webster, *The Church of Rome at the Bar of History* (Edinburgh: Banner of Truth Trust, 1995), 41.

4. Ibid., 49.

5. Alexander Hislop, *The Two Babylons*, 2nd ed. (Ontario, CA: Chick Publications, 1998), 83–86.

6. I.A. Sadler, *Mystery Babylon the Great* (Reading, UK: I. A. Sadler, 2002), 103.

APPENDIX M

PRIESTCRAFT – THE HIDDEN
RELIGION OF CONTROL

How Clerical Power Replaced Christ's Headship and Hijacked the Gospel

> *"Beware of false prophets, who come to you in sheep's clothing but inwardly are ravenous wolves."*
> *(Matthew 7:15).*

> *"The priests did not ask, "Where is the LORD?"... they handled the law but did not know Me." (Jeremiah 2:8).*

Priestcraft isn't biblical Christianity. It's the ancient art of religious control—disguised as holiness, enforced by fear, and legitimized by robes, rituals, and rank.

From Babylon to Rome, and from Rome to modern megachurches, priestcraft has followed one goal: to insert a human intermediary between God and man. It thrives wherever authority is exalted over access, and tradition replaces transformation.

What's Priestcraft?

Definition: The manipulation of religion by a clerical class to gain power, enforce submission, and mediate access to God—usually through ritual, mysticism, or institutional hierarchy.[1] Priestcraft is when:

- Men claim to dispense grace
- Leaders demand obedience to their title
- People are taught to fear questioning the clergy
- Salvation is tied to the structure, not the Savior

Biblical Christianity Versus Priestcraft

Biblical Christianity teaches:

- Jesus is the only Mediator (1 Timothy 2:5)
- Every believer is a priest (1 Peter 2:9)
- Authority is based on servanthood, not status (Matthew 23:11–12)
- The Holy Spirit leads individuals into all truth (John 16:13)

Priestcraft teaches:

- Access to God must be filtered through men
- Spiritual knowledge is reserved for the clergy
- Disobedience to church leaders equals rebellion against God

- Traditions of men carry more weight than Scripture

The Roots of Priestcraft

- **Babylon:** Priest-kings served as mediators between the gods and the people.
- **Egypt:** Priests of Horus and Isis controlled political power through mysticism.
- **Rome:** The title *Pontifex Maximus*—a priest-emperor hybrid.
- **Pharisees:** Religious experts who blocked access to God with tradition (Matthew 23:13).

Rome didn't destroy these models—it perfected them in the form of the papacy.

The Modern Face of Priestcraft

It's not just in Catholicism. Today, priestcraft has evolved to include:

- Charismatic "apostles" who demand blind submission
- Seminaries that grant spiritual authority based on credentials, not calling
- Mega-church CEOs who rule through image and branding
- Prosperity preachers who monetize access to miracles

It doesn't matter the label—when man inserts himself between you and Christ, priestcraft is at work.

Why God Hates It

"There is one God and one Mediator between God and mankind, the man Christ Jesus." (1 Timothy 2:5).

Priestcraft:

- Rebuilds the veil Jesus tore
- Replaces intimacy with intercession by hierarchy
- Robs Christ of His finished work
- Creates spiritual dependence on men instead of the Spirit

If You've Been Under Priestcraft...

You may feel:

- Spiritually stunted
- Intimidated to ask questions
- Guilty for leaving a church or challenging a leader
- Confused about grace, salvation, or your spiritual gifts

This isn't just emotional trauma—it's spiritual bondage.

How to Break Free

- Recognize that priestcraft is a counterfeit.
- Repent of any agreement you made with false religious authority.
- Forgive those who used religion to control you.
- Renounce the belief that access to God comes through men.
- Reclaim your identity as a child of God and royal priest.

- Follow Christ directly—through His Word, His Spirit, and His finished work.

Final Word

You don't need a priest to approach God. You don't need permission to be free. You don't need robes, relics, or rituals. You need Jesus.

> *"You have an anointing from the Holy One, and you all know the truth." (1 John 2:20).*

> *"Where the Spirit of the Lord is, there is freedom." (2 Corinthians 3:17).*

Tear down the altar of man. Walk boldly into the throne room. And never bow to priestcraft again.

Notes

1. Based on historical and theological analysis in *The Two Babylons* by Alexander Hislop and *A Woman Rides the Beast* by Dave Hunt.

APPENDIX N

PETER'S BONES AND THE
VATICAN BURIAL HOAX

The Greatest Cover-Up Never Told

> *"He is not here; He has risen, just as He said. Come, see the place where He lay." (Matthew 28:6).*

> *"We cannot do anything against the truth, but only for the truth." (2 Corinthians 13:8).*

For centuries, the Roman Catholic Church has taught that the apostle Peter was martyred in Rome and that his tomb lies beneath St. Peter's Basilica. This tradition has shaped ecclesiastical claims of apostolic succession and spiritual authority. A monument was built over it. A basilica was raised above it. A religious empire grounded its authority in it.

But there's a critical distinction that must be made: the claim is not conclusively supported by the archaeological evidence.

If Peter is not buried in Rome, then the Vatican's claim to territorial apostolic succession and Petrine supremacy is weakened at its historical root. The issue is not devotion; it's foundational.

As Scripture reminds us:

> *"For no one can lay any foundation other than what has been laid down. That foundation is Jesus Christ"* (1 Corinthians 3:11).

The Tomb Tradition at St. Peter's

According to longstanding Catholic tradition, Peter was crucified upside down in Rome under Emperor Nero around AD 64 and buried on Vatican Hill.[1] The belief that Peter's body rests beneath the basilica is deeply intertwined with Rome's claim that the Bishop of Rome inherits Peter's authority.

The earliest textual witness to a Roman memorial comes from the presbyter Gaius, writing around the turn of the third century, who referred to the "trophy" (tropaion) of Peter at the Vatican.[2] This indicates that by the late second century, a site was being venerated in Rome as associated with Peter.

Archaeology confirms that a burial area on Vatican Hill was venerated by Christians by the second century. What archaeology does not confirm with certainty is that any specific bones discovered there belong to the apostle Peter.

Those are two very different conclusions.

The 20th-Century Excavations

In 1939, excavations began beneath St. Peter's Basilica under the direction of Jesuit archaeologist Antonio Ferrua.[3] The dig revealed:

- A Roman necropolis containing multiple pagan mausoleums.
- A second-century memorial structure commonly identified with the "Trophy of Gaius."[2]
- Aedicula-style shrine construction, later incorporated into Constantine's fourth-century basilica.[4]
- Multiple human bone fragments in nearby niches.
- Pagan tombs and extensive graffiti.
- No burial inscription naming Peter.
- No uncontested forensic identification.

Excavators also reported that the soil directly beneath the aedicula showed no clear, undisturbed primary burial cavity attributable to Peter.[3]

These findings demonstrate early veneration. They do not demonstrate definitive identification.

In 1950, Pope Pius XII publicly declared, "The tomb of the Prince of the Apostles has been found."[5] It was meant to serve as proof of Rome's divine right to lead the global Church. The declaration exceeded what the archaeological evidence could conclusively establish.

The Graffiti Wall and the Bones

During excavation, bones were mysteriously discovered in a niche within what became known as the "graffiti wall," separate from the central burial cavity. The Vatican later commissioned classical epigrapher Margherita Guarducci to study the graffiti inscriptions. Her interpretation differed significantly from the earlier caution expressed by Antonio Ferrua. Guarducci later argued that nearby inscriptions — including partial graffiti interpreted as PETR...

ENI... ("Peter is here") — supported identification of the bones as Peter's.[6]

She also reported that scientific examination indicated the bones had once been wrapped in purple-dyed cloth interwoven with gold thread — details she interpreted as signs of veneration befitting an apostle.[6]

However:

- The bones were not found in the original burial cavity.[3]
- The fragments came from multiple individuals.[3]
- Animal bones (including sheep, ox, pig, and mouse) were reportedly present in the same collection.[3]
- No inscription directly naming Peter was found.
- No DNA confirmation exists.

Antonio Ferrua himself expressed reservations about definitively linking any specific remains to the apostle.[3] And yet, these unverified fragments are now enshrined and paraded as holy relics.

Nevertheless, in 1968, Pope Paul VI declared that the relics could be considered Peter's remains.[7] This is the central issue: interpretive probability was elevated to institutional certainty.

Ed Kurath observes that religious systems often replace scriptural foundation with inherited structure when tradition becomes insulated from scrutiny.[8] The question here is not whether Christians honored Peter. The question is whether institutional authority rests on demonstrable evidence or an inherited assumption.

Other authors and investigators have suggested that the timing and presentation of the discovery raise legitimate questions about institutional motivation. Protestant researcher Dave Hunt argues that the Vatican had enormous symbolic stakes tied to proving

Peter's burial in Rome and notes that the more cautious conclusions of early excavators were later overshadowed by Margherita Guarducci's confident identification of the remains.[9]

Former Catholic historian Peter De Rosa likewise observes that papal authority has long been intertwined with the physical symbolism of Peter's tomb, and that institutional declarations have sometimes exceeded the limits of available historical evidence.[10]

Journalist John Walsh presents the tension between Ferrua and Guarducci in a way that supports the idea of interpretive shift without alleging fraud.[3]

Some evangelical commentators have further suggested that once Pope Pius XII publicly linked the excavation to Petrine legitimacy, the pressure for a definitive identification intensified.

While none of these authors present documentary proof of coercion or fabrication, they argue that the alignment between ecclesiastical need and archaeological interpretation has fueled enduring skepticism about the certainty of the Vatican's claims.

Constantine and the Monumentalization of Memory

In the fourth century, Emperor Constantine ordered the construction of a massive basilica over the site. Vatican Hill was leveled in an extraordinary engineering project to build the Constantinian basilica directly above the memorial structure.[4]

Eusebius confirms Peter's martyrdom but does not provide archaeological confirmation of his burial site.[2] Jerome repeats the martyrdom tradition but likewise provides no forensic detail.[11]

The existence of a monumental church demonstrates the strength of tradition, not the certainty of identification.

When theological authority becomes geographically anchored — tied to a specific tomb — historical certainty becomes foundational to institutional legitimacy.

The Lateran Complication

Another layer of complexity further clouds the issue.

Catholic tradition holds that the heads of Peter and Paul were later separated from their bodies and transferred for protection. Today, the skull relics of Peter and Paul are displayed in reliquaries above the papal altar in the Basilica of St. John Lateran — not in St. Peter's Basilica.[12]

In medieval relic theology and Roman legal tradition, the head was often regarded as the primary relic. If the heads are venerated at the Lateran — the cathedral of the Bishop of Rome — then the burial narrative centered exclusively at St. Peter's Basilica becomes more complex than commonly presented.[12]

Alternative Burial Theories

Some researchers have proposed alternative burial locations, including Jerusalem near the Mount of Olives.[13] Archaeologist Charles Clermont-Ganneau (1873) and later Bellarmino Bagatti reported the discovery of ossuaries bearing New Testament-era names in early Christian burial sites in Jerusalem.[14]

Among the inscriptions discussed in this context is "Shimon bar Yonah," the full Hebrew form of Peter's name.[14]

These interpretations remain highly contested in mainstream scholarship. They do not conclusively establish that Peter was buried in Jerusalem. They do, however, demonstrate that the burial question is not universally settled.

Some accounts allege that Bagatti's findings were not widely publicized, and journalist Tom Mueller describes the tensions surrounding Petrine relic claims in his reporting on the Vatican excavations.[15] Such claims remain debated and lack universally accepted documentary confirmation.

The point is not to prove Jerusalem. The point is to demonstrate that Rome is not conclusively proven, and if Peter is not buried in Rome, the foundation for papal supremacy crumbles.

Scripture and Silence

There is no biblical evidence that Peter ever traveled to Rome. Paul's letter to the Romans doesn't mention Peter—despite listing 27 names (Romans 16).

The book of Acts follows Peter's ministry extensively but never records his arrival in Rome.

When Paul wrote from Roman imprisonment, he stated: "At my first defense, no one stood with me" (2 Timothy 4:16). Wouldn't Peter have been there—if he was bishop of Rome?

Furthermore, Jesus — not Peter — is called the Cornerstone (1 Corinthians 3:11; Ephesians 2:20). Peter's confession of Christ is foundational, but Scripture never describes him as a monarchal bishop ruling from Rome.

If papal supremacy historically rests on Peter's burial in Rome, and that burial remains archaeologically inconclusive, then the historical foundation of universal jurisdiction warrants reexamination.

Final Assessment

Archaeology shows:

- Early veneration.
- A second-century memorial.
- Bones in proximity to that shrine.
- Interpretive inscriptions.
- No definitive identification.

- No uncontested forensic proof.
- The Vatican presents certainty.
- The archaeology presents probability at best.

That gap matters.

The Vatican's claim to Peter's bones isn't supported by:

- Scripture
- History
- Archaeology
- The early Church fathers

Neither contemporary inscription nor uncontested forensic evidence exists in the public archaeological record to confirm that these fragments are Peter's.[3] The issue is not devotion to Peter. The issue is authority grounded in certainty, where evidence remains debated.

It's a myth turned dogma. A symbol of power built on sand. And if they lied about Peter's burial, what else have they buried?

Notes

1. Jerome, *De Viris Illustribus*, 1; Eusebius, *Ecclesiastical History*, 2.25.

2. Eusebius, *Ecclesiastical History*, 2.25.

3. John Evangelist Walsh, *The Bones of Saint Peter* (New York: Image Books, 1985), 129–150.

4. Eusebius, *Life of Constantine*, 3.25–40; Ramsay MacMullen, *Christianity and Paganism in the Fourth to Eighth Centuries* (New Haven: Yale University Press, 1997), 74–76.

5. Pope Pius XII, Radio Address, December 23, 1950.

6. Margherita Guarducci, *The Tomb of St. Peter* (New York: Hawthorn Books, 1960).

7. Pope Paul VI, General Audience, June 26, 1968.

8. Ed Kurath, *I Will Give You Rest* (Post Falls, ID: Divinely Designed, 2003), chap. 6.

9. Dave Hunt, *A Woman Rides the Beast: The Roman Catholic Church and the Last Days* (Eugene, OR: Harvest House Publishers, 1994), 220–225.

10. Peter De Rosa, *Vicars of Christ: The Dark Side of the Papacy* (New York: Crown Publishers, 1988), 33–40.

11. Jerome, *Commentary on Matthew*, in *Patrologia Latina*, vol. 26, ed. J.-P. Migne (Paris: 1844–1864)

12. Peter De Rosa, *Vicars of Christ* (New York: Crown Publishers, 1988), 37–39.

13. Charles Clermont-Ganneau, "Jewish-Christian Tombs on the Mount of Olives," *Palestine Exploration Fund Quarterly Statement* 5 (1873): 122–132.

14. Bellarmino Bagatti, "Recent Discoveries in the Field of Christian Archaeology," *Studium Biblicum Franciscanum Liber Annuus* 22 (1972): 5–38.

15. Walsh, *Bones of Saint Peter*, 171–179.

APPENDIX O

GLOSSARY OF PAGAN
TERMS IN CHRISTIANITY

Understanding the Origins of Ritual, Language, and Belief Systems

> *"Let no one take you captive through philosophy and*
> *empty deception, according to the tradition of men."*
> *(Colossians 2:8).*

> *"The customs of the peoples are worthless." (Jeremiah*
> *10:3).*

Many terms used in modern Christianity—especially within Catholicism and high-Protestant traditions—are not found in Scripture and don't originate in the teachings of Jesus or His apostles. They come from Babylon, Rome, and Greek philosophical systems.

This glossary isn't intended for legalistic or condemnatory purposes. It's a tool of discernment—to help you recognize how language has been used to smuggle in false religion.

Mass

Origin: Latin *missa*, related to dismissal or sacrifice; tied to Roman Catholic Eucharistic sacrifice

Biblical Contrast: The Lord's Supper is a remembrance, not a repeated sacrifice (Luke 22:19; Hebrews 10:10–14)

Easter

Origin: Derived from *Eostre*, a Germanic fertility goddess

Biblical Contrast: Passover (Pesach) is the biblical commemoration (Exodus 12; Luke 22:15)

Sacrament

Origin: Latin *sacramentum*, used in Roman military oaths

Biblical Contrast: Baptism and the Lord's Supper are acts of obedience, not mystical rites (Romans 6:3–4; 1 Corinthians 11:24–26)

Lent

Origin: From Anglo-Saxon *lencten* (spring); rooted in preChristian fasting rituals

Biblical Contrast: New Testament fasting is voluntary and Spirit-led (Matthew 6:16–18)

Priest (New Covenant context)

Origin: Derived from Old Covenant temple system and pagan mediator roles

Biblical Contrast: All believers are priests (1 Peter 2:9); Jesus is our High Priest (Hebrews 4:14–16)

Holy Father

Origin: Pagan Rome used similar titles for emperors; also used for Jupiter

Biblical Contrast: Jesus said to call no man "father" in a spiritual sense (Matthew 23:9)

Cathedral

Origin: From Latin *cathedra* (seat of authority), linked to imperial rule

Biblical Contrast: The early Church met in homes and had no central governing seats (Acts 2:46; Romans 16:5)

Confirmation

Origin: Modeled after Roman coming-of-age rites

Biblical Contrast: The Holy Spirit is received at new birth, not by institutional ceremony (Acts 2:38; Galatians 3:2)

Advent

Origin: Latin *adventus*, meaning "arrival," based on ancient imperial celebrations

Biblical Contrast: Believers await Christ's return, not reenact seasonal liturgy (Titus 2:13)

Clergy / Laity

Origin: Greek *kleros* (lot) vs. *laos* (people); developed into a hierarchy

Biblical Contrast: The New Testament shows a shared priesthood and mutual service (1 Peter 2:5; Ephesians 4:11–13)

Why This Matters

Language shapes belief. If we casually adopt words and concepts without understanding their origins, we risk:

- Repeating empty rituals

- Inheriting deception
- Calling holy what God never ordained

The gospel isn't built on pagan terms. It's built on a crucified and risen Savior.

> *"You nullify the word of God by your tradition that you have handed down. And you do many other similar things." (Mark 7:13).*

> *"Test everything; hold fast to what is good." (1 Thessalonians 5:21).*

Let your words reflect your worship. And let your worship reflect the Word.

APPENDIX P

CONSTANTINE'S TIMELINE AND
THE SERPENT'S ARCHITECTURE

From Roman Power to Vatican Serpent Imagery—A Prophetic Overview

"By their fruit you will recognize them." (Matthew 7:16).

*"Have nothing to do with the fruitless deeds of darkness,
but rather expose them." (Ephesians 5:11).*

This appendix traces the transformation of Christianity from a Spiritled movement to a state-controlled institution—one infused with pagan ideology, Roman imperialism, and serpent symbolism. It exposes both the historical corruption under Constantine and the visual evidence of spiritual deception embedded in Vatican architecture today.

Constantine's Timeline: How Power Replaced Purity

- **272**: Birth of Constantine the Great. Born into Roman power, Constantine would later merge the empire with the Church.
- **312**: The Battle of the Milvian Bridge. Constantine sees a vision: a cross and the phrase "In this sign, conquer." The cross becomes a symbol of state-sanctioned domination.
- **313**: The Edict of Milan. Christianity is legalized. The persecuted Church becomes politically protected—but also vulnerable to compromise.
- **321**: Constantine declares Sunday the legal day of worship. To honor the sun god, Constantine formalizes Sunday worship, replacing the biblical Sabbath. Syncretism begins.
- **325**: The Council of Nicaea. The first ecumenical council unifies doctrine under imperial control. Core issues such as sanctification and spiritual warfare are sidelined.
- **330**: Constantinople becomes the new Rome. A new imperial capital is built on Christian symbolism—but still rooted in Caesar's structure.
- **381**: Christianity becomes the state religion. Emperor Theodosius makes Christianity the only legal religion. Pagan temples are closed, but their practices live on inside Church walls.
- **431**: The Council of Ephesus: Mary is officially titled *Theotokos* ("Mother of God"). Marian veneration rises as goddess worship is rebranded.
- **590**: Pope Gregory I consolidates papal power. Hierarchy solidifies. Clergy dominate. Rome becomes not just the spiritual center—but the new Caesar's throne.

- **1054**: The Great Schism. Eastern and Western Christianity divide. The Roman Catholic Church continues with Constantine's legacy: hierarchy, syncretism, and institutional control.

Why This Timeline Still Matters

The Church Christ founded was:

- Spirit-led
- Ground-level (grassroots, non-hierarchical)
- Free from political control

The Church Constantine established became:

- Hierarchical
- Imperial
- Bound by tradition, wealth, and power

This isn't just historical—it's spiritual. It's the root of the Constantine Curse: a church built by Rome, not by Christ.

The Serpent's Architecture: What's Hiding in Plain Sight

This is where my follow-up book to this one, *The False Christ of Rome,* begins.

When you look past the theology and into the architecture, artwork, and design of the modern Church—especially in Rome — you find the fingerprints of something not just unbiblical . . . but Luciferian.

Paul VI Audience Hall (1971)

Located inside Vatican City, this building:

- Resembles a serpent's head from the outside
- Features curved windows as reptilian eyes
- Contains a throne platform resembling a serpent's mouth and tongue

Behind the pope's seat is a twisted bronze sculpture titled *The Resurrection*, depicting Christ emerging from nuclear chaos. But to many, it looks more like a demonic entity rising from the underworld.

Other Vatican Symbols with Pagan or Occult Roots

- **Obelisk in St. Peter's Square:** Symbol of Baal worship, originally from Egypt.
- **Dagon fish miter:** Hat design adopted from Philistine fish god.
- **Sunburst monstrance:** Solar deity imagery used for Eucharistic adoration.
- **Pine cone staff:** Symbol of Osiris, fertility, and third-eye awakening.

These aren't mistakes. They're messages—spiritual declarations embedded in stone.

Symbols Aren't Neutral

God warned against carved images and pagan customs for a reason: the enemy speaks through architecture, geometry, color, and ritual. The Vatican isn't just religious—it's esoteric.

"She has become a haunt for demons . . . For all the nations have drunk the wine of her immorality." (Revelation 18:2–3).

APPENDIX Q

THE FINAL DEFENSE: WHY THE CHURCH
CANNOT BE SAVED FROM WITHIN

The Catholic Rebuttal to Catholicism's Own Collapse

Even some of the Church's most vocal traditionalist defenders, including Taylor Marshall, have argued that the modern Catholic Church has been seriously compromised by ideological and institutional infiltration. In *Infiltration: The Plot to Destroy the Church from Within*, Marshall contends that hostile forces — including Freemasonic and secular globalist movements — sought to exert influence within the Church's hierarchy, particularly in the nineteenth and twentieth centuries.[1]

Marshall documents concerns about internal corruption, doctrinal ambiguity, and clerical misconduct. Yet his proposed solution is not separation from Rome, but reform from within. He urges Catholics to remain, resist error, and reclaim the Church's historic orthodoxy.

This creates a tension that cannot be ignored.

If the institutional structure itself has been compromised at the highest levels, can it be repaired by those who remain subject to its authority?

Sidebar: A Catholic's Own Case for Infiltration

Marshall writes:

"The secret societies of Europe, particularly the Freemasons, were hell-bent on penetrating and corrupting the Catholic Church from within. They weren't trying to destroy the Church from the outside. They wanted to sit on Peter's Chair."[1]

He cites the 19th-century **Alta Vendita** document—an open conspiracy by Masonic lodges to subvert the Church by installing a Pope who would forward their agenda:

"We must have a Pope according to our needs... With that, we shall march more securely toward the assault on the Church than with the pamphlets of our brethren in France and the gold of England."[2]

Even **Pope Leo XIII**, in 1884, warned that Freemasonry was not just a political threat—but a satanic one:

"A satanic sect bent on overturning the entire order of Christendom."[3]

And more recently, **Archbishop Carlo Maria Viganò**, former Vatican ambassador to the U.S., sounded the same alarm:

"The deep state is mirrored by a deep Church, filled with traitors who no longer serve Christ but serve globalist and Luciferian agendas."[4]

These are not accusations made by Protestant critics. They are voiced by Catholics themselves.

But What Is the Catholic Response?

The Vatican is burning, yet the apologists stand inside it with fire hoses and false hope:

- "The Church is both human and divine."
- "She is wounded but still holy."
- "We can clean house and save her."

To this, we respond:

"Yes, the house is on fire — but if we kick out the arsonists, we can save the cathedral."

But his call to "save the Church" is like trying to clean the inside of the **Titanic** while it's sinking.

If even Taylor Marshall admits the Vatican has been infiltrated by **Freemasons, globalists, and Luciferian agents...**

Then what exactly are Catholics defending?

You don't patch up a corpse.

You bury it.

Or better yet — you walk out of the tomb.

Notes

1. Taylor Marshall, *Infiltration: The Plot to Destroy the Church from Within* (Manchester, NH: Sophia Institute Press, 2019), 80.

2. *The Permanent Instruction of the Alta Vendita*, cited in Marshall, *Infiltration*, 103.

3. Leo XIII, *Humanum Genus*, April 20, 1884.

4. Carlo Maria Viganò, "Open Letter to President Donald Trump," October 25, 2020.

APPENDIX R
KEY VISUALS AND IMAGE REFERENCES

*The following credits document the sources and copyright status
of all visual materials used throughout this book. All images are
in the public domain or used under appropriate licensing.*

Vision of the Cross —
Fresco by Raphael's workshop, Vatican Museums (c. 1520–1524).
Public domain image via Wikimedia Commons.
Source: https://commons.wikimedia.org/wiki/File:Raphael_Vi
sion_Cross.jpg

St. Peter's Dome and Pantheon Dome —
Comparison of two domes reflecting imperial architecture:

- **Top:** *Cupola of St. Peter's Basilica*, Vatican.

Photo by Livioandronico2013. Wikimedia Commons. Licensed
under CC BY-SA 4.0.

Source: https://commons.wikimedia.org/wiki/File:Cupola_di_San_Pietro.jpg

- **Bottom:** *Pantheon Dome*, Rome.

Photo by Jean-Christophe Benoist. Wikimedia Commons. Licensed under CC BY-SA 3.0.
Source: https://commons.wikimedia.org/wiki/File:Pantheon_(Rome)_Dome_interior.jpg

The Seven Sacraments: Catholic Infographic —
Diagram titled *"The Seven Sacraments"* by Felix Just, S.J., Ph.D.
Public domain image via Catholic-Resources.org. Accessed 2025.
Source: https://catholic-resources.org/ChurchDocs/Sacraments.htm

Tribunal de la Inquisición —
Painting by Francisco de Goya (c. 1812–1819), depicting the brutality of the Spanish Inquisition.
Public domain image via Wikimedia Commons.
Source: https://commons.wikimedia.org/wiki/File:Tribunal_de_la_Inquisición.jpg

Constantine I Coin with Sol Invictus —
Roman coin issued under Emperor Constantine I (c. 337 AD), featuring the pagan deity Sol Invictus despite Constantine's public alignment with Christianity.
Public domain image via Wikimedia Commons.
Source: https://commons.wikimedia.org/wiki/File:Follis-Constantine-lyons_RIC_VI_309.jpg

Mithraeum beneath Basilica of San Clemente —

Image depicting the subterranean Mithraeum (pagan temple of Mithras) located beneath the layered archaeological site of the Basilica of San Clemente in Rome.

Public domain image via Wikimedia Commons.

Source: https://commons.wikimedia.org/wiki/File:San_Clemente_Mithraeum.jpg

Arch of Constantine with Pagan Medallions —

Photo of the Arch of Constantine in Rome (completed in 315 AD), featuring reused medallions of the sun god Sol and moon goddess Luna integrated into its imperial Christian reliefs.

Adapted from *"Arch of Constantine: The Monument With Many Faces"* by Vedran Bileta (TheCollector), via Wikimedia Commons. Public domain image.

Source: https://commons.wikimedia.org/wiki/File:Arch_of_Constantine_-_015.jpg

The Parable of the Wise and Foolish Builders —

Illustration showing the collapse of the house built on sand, based on Jesus's teaching in Matthew 7:26–27.

Image by FreeBibleImages, Good News Productions International & College Press Publishing. Licensed under CC BY-NC-ND 4.0.

Downloaded from www.freebibleimages.org

The Whore of Babylon: Modern Interpretation —

Modern digital artwork inspired by Hans Burgkmair the Elder's 1523 woodcut *The Whore of Babylon*, based on Revelation 17.

This adaptation incorporates updated color, symbolism, and graphic overlays while preserving the visual theme of spiritual seduction, occultism, and imperial corruption.

The original image is in the public domain; the adaptation circulated via Wikimedia Commons, The Christian Post, and public prophecy archives. Artist unknown.

Source (variant image): https://commons.wikimedia.org/wiki/File:Burgkmair_whore_babylon_color.jpg

Note: Modern reinterpretation; included under public domain derivative use.

Petros vs. Petra: Matthew 16:18 Greek Comparison —

Educational diagram adapted from *"The Great Confession"*, SlidePlayer.

This image compares the Koine Greek words *Petros* (Peter) and *Petra* (bedrock) to challenge traditional papal interpretations of Matthew 16:18.

Source materials include:

- BibleHub Greek interlinear
- Pinterest theology slides
- Wikimedia Commons
- SlidePlayer theology decks

AI-Generated Illustration: Created by the author using OpenAI image generation technology. This image was generated specifically for this work and is not derived from any copyrighted source.

Vatican Necropolis Excavation Beneath St. Peter's Basilica —

Photograph of Roman-era burial chambers discovered beneath St. Peter's Basilica during the 1940–1949 Vatican-sponsored archaeological excavations.

Public domain image via Wikimedia Commons.

Source: https://en.wikipedia.org/wiki/Vatican_Necropolis#/media/File:Vatican_Necropolis_tomb.jpg

Christ the Good Shepherd Mosaic —

5th-century mosaic from the Mausoleum of Galla Placidia, Ravenna, depicting Christ as the Good Shepherd among His flock. Early Christian imagery consistently presents Christ Himself—not an apostle or institutional office—as the foundation and shepherd of the Church, aligning with New Testament teaching that *"no one can lay a foundation other than the one already laid, which is Jesus Christ"* (1 Corinthians 3:11; cf. Ephesians 2:20).

Public domain image via Wikimedia Commons.

Source: https://commons.wikimedia.org/wiki/File:%22The_good_Shepherd%22_mosaic_-_Mausoleum_of_Galla_Placidia.jpg

Greek Philosopher Busts —

Marble busts of Plato, Socrates, and Aristotle from various museum collections. These figures shaped classical thought and later influenced Christian theology—especially through Augustine and Aquinas—embedding philosophical frameworks into doctrines of God, soul, and salvation. Sources:

- *Plato*: Altes Museum, Berlin – public domain.
- *Socrates*: Photo by Luciusmichael, via Wikimedia Commons – public domain.
- *Aristotle*: From the Ludovisi Collection, Museo Nazionale Romano – public domain.

Composite image curated for educational commentary.

George Fox Preaching in Maryland —

17th-century woodcut engraving depicting George Fox delivering a sermon beneath an oak tree in Maryland. His radical Quaker message emphasized the "Inner Light" of Christ within each person and rejected institutional religion. Originally circulated in 19th-century Quaker publications and tracts promoting Spirit-led faith.

Public domain via Wikimedia Commons.

Image credit: *George Fox preaching in Maryland*. Illustrator unknown.

Pontifex Maximus Inscription —

Photograph of an ancient Roman inscription slab bearing the abbreviation "PONT MAX," short for *Pontifex Maximus*, the chief high priest of Rome's pagan religion.

Public domain via Wikimedia Commons.

Source: https://commons.wikimedia.org/wiki/File:Ara_a_Tib%C3%A9rio_Cl%C3%A1udio_MNArqueologia.tif

Execution of William Tyndale —

Woodcut illustration from *Foxe's Book of Martyrs* (1563), showing the execution of William Tyndale by strangulation and burning in Vilvoorde, Belgium. Tyndale's only crime: translating the New Testament into English.

Source: *Foxe's Book of Martyrs* (public domain), as archived by World History Encyclopedia. https://www.worldhistory.org/image/15560/execution-of-william-tyndale/

Council of Nicaea —

Painting by Pavlovskyi, Maksimovych, Galik & Karataev, housed in the Gate Church of the Trinity, Kyiv Pechersk Lavra (Ukraine). This 18th-century artwork illustrates the first ecumenical council convened under Emperor Constantine's direction in AD 325, which formally aligned Christian doctrine with imperial authority.

Public domain via Wikimedia Commons.

Source: https://commons.wikimedia.org/wiki/File:THE_FIRST_COUNCIL_OF_NICEA.jpg

St. Peter's Obelisk —

Photograph of the Egyptian obelisk in the center of St. Peter's Square, Vatican City. Originally brought from Heliopolis, Egypt, to Rome by Emperor Caligula, it stood near the Circus of Nero, where early Christians were martyred. Re-erected in its current position in 1586 by Pope Sixtus V as a symbol of Rome's fusion of pagan and Christian power.

Photo by Jebulon, 2013, Public domain (CC0).

Source: https://commons.wikimedia.org/wiki/File:St.Peters Basilica.JPG

Crux Quadrata —

Early Christian crux quadrata (equal-armed cross), 5th-century mosaic from the Mausoleum of Galla Placidia, Ravenna. Used prominently in post-Constantinian Christian iconography. The equal-armed design symbolized symmetry, state order, and unity— often used in mosaics and Church seals.

Image credit: Crux quadrata (Greek equal-armed cross diagram). Public domain via Wikimedia Commons

Source: https://commons.wikimedia.org/w/index.php?search=Mausoleum+of+Galla+Placidia&title=Special%3AMediaSearch&type=image

Lateran Treaty Group Portrait —

Vintage group image of Vatican and Italian government officials inside the Lateran Palace just prior to signing the Lateran Treaty on February 11, 1929.

Public domain via Wikimedia Commons

Source: https://commons.wikimedia.org/wiki/File:Group_of_Vatican_and_Italian_government_notables_posing_at_the_Lateran_Palace_before_the_signing_of_the_treaty.jpg

World Day of Prayer for Peace Memorial —

Photo of *World Day of Prayer for Peace* bronze engraving by Chris Light, located in Assisi, Italy.

Public domain via Wikimedia Commons

Licensed under CC BY-SA 4.0.

Source: https://commons.wikimedia.org/wiki/File:Peace_Conference_10-11_489.jpg

Document on Human Fraternity Signing —

Public domain photo via *Vatican News*, showing Pope Francis and Sheikh Ahmed el-Tayeb signing the *Document on Human Fraternity* in 2019. Widely circulated by official Vatican and interfaith platforms, including *Our Sunday Visitor* and https://www.vaticannews.va/en/pope/news/2019-02/pope-francis-uae-declaration-with-al-azhar-grand-imam.html

Jesuit IHS Monogram —

Public domain graphic of the official seal of the Society of Jesus (Jesuits), showing the IHS Christogram encircled by a sunburst. Image credited to Moranski, widely circulated in academic and ecclesiastical publications.

Public domain via Wikimedia Commons

Source: https://commons.wikimedia.org/wiki/File:Jesuit%27s_Great_Seal_With_The_Monogram_Of_Jesus.jpg

Catholic Clergy Procession —

Photograph of Catholic bishops and clergy in ceremonial regalia (scarlet, purple, and gold) at the ordination of Bishop Fülöp Kocsis in Hajdúdorog, Hungary. Public domain photo by Jojojoe.

Public domain via Wikimedia Commons

Source: https://commons.wikimedia.org/wiki/File:Ordain ing_F%C3%BCl%C3%B6p_bishop_of_Hajdudorog.jpg

Papal Tiara Display —

Photograph of Pope Paul VI's tiara and stole, displayed at the Basilica of the National Shrine of the Immaculate Conception in Washington, D.C. (1968). These ceremonial vestments were used in coronation rituals prior to Vatican II.

Public domain via Wikimedia Commons

Source: https://commons.wikimedia.org/wiki/File:788Bergamo TiaraGiovanniXXIII.jpg

Confessional Booth: Chapel of Saint Anne (France) —

Wooden confessional illustrating the institutionalization of priest-mediated absolution within Roman Catholic practice. The confessional system formalized a model of forgiveness that placed clerical authority between the believer and God—contrasting with the New Testament teaching that forgiveness and reconciliation come directly through Jesus Christ (1 Timothy 2:5; Hebrews 4:16).

Public domain via Wikimedia Commons

Source: https://commons.wikimedia.org/wiki/File:Confession nal_chapelle_Sainte-Anne.jpg

Pope Benedict XVI Elevating the Host —

Photograph of Pope Benedict XVI holding up the Eucharistic

wafer during a Catholic Mass, illustrating the doctrine of transubstantiation and Rome's repeated sacrificial ritual.

Photo by Fabio Pozzebom / Agência Brasil; licensed under CC BY 3.0 Brazil.

Source: https://en.wikipedia.org/wiki/Sacramentum_caritatis#/media/File:BentoXVI-51-11052007_(frag).jpg

Madonna and Child Enthroned with Angels —

Workshop of Bernardino Luini (c. early 16th century).

This Renaissance depiction reflects the development of Marian enthronement imagery within late medieval and early modern Catholic art, portraying Mary as a regal, mediating figure seated above the faithful. Such visual theology parallels the Church's growing emphasis on Marian intercession and queenship—concepts that extend beyond the New Testament's presentation of Mary as a humble servant of God (Luke 1:38).

Public domain via Wikimedia Commons

Source: https://commons.wikimedia.org/wiki/File:Brooklyn_Museum_-_Madonna_and_Child_Enthroned_with_Angels_-_Workshop_of_Bernardino_Luini.jpg

Antichrist Fresco —

Luca Signorelli, fresco fragment from *The Antichrist* series (1499– 1504), Cappella Nuova, Orvieto Cathedral.

Public domain via Wikimedia Commons

Source: https://commons.wikimedia.org/wiki/File:Signorelli-Antichrist_and_the_devil.jpg

Mary Procession —

Statues of Our Lady of Grace (Miraculous Medal), Philippines:

Multiple statues of Our Lady of Grace, the Marian figure associated with the Miraculous Medal devotion, are displayed in public devotional settings in the Philippines. The imagery reflects the global spread and localization of Marian devotion originating from 19th-century France, emphasizing Mary as a channel of grace and intercessory power. This visual repetition illustrates how Miraculous Medal symbolism—rays of grace, Marian mediation, and devotional posture—has been replicated worldwide in modern Catholic devotional practice.

Public domain via Wikimedia Commons

Source: https://commons.wikimedia.org/wiki/File:Statues_of_Our_Lady_of_Grace_(Miraculous_Medal)_in_the_Philippines_01.jpg

Virgin Mary Crowned by Two Angels —

Albrecht Dürer (1471–1528), *Virgin Mary Crowned by Two Angels*, engraving, 1518. Public domain image via Wikimedia Commons.

Public domain via Wikimedia Commons

Source: https://commons.wikimedia.org/wiki/File:Virgin_and_Child_Crowned_by_Two_Angels_MET_DP815894.jpg

Isis Nursing Horus —

Illustration from *A History of Art in Ancient Egypt* by Georges Perrot and Charles Chipiez, published 1883, depicting the Egyptian goddess Isis nursing the child Horus.

Public domain via Wikimedia Commons.

Source: https://commons.wikimedia.org/wiki/File:A_history_of_art_in_ancient_Egypt_(1883)_(14769397631).jpg

Virgin Nursing the Christ Child (Virgo Lactans) —

Unknown artist, tempera on panel, 14th century, depicting the Virgin Mary nursing the Christ Child.

Public domain. North Carolina Museum of Art Open Access Collection.

Source: https://collection.ncartmuseum.org/objects/441/the-virgin-nursing-the-christ-child

Our Lady of Fátima Statue —
Sculpture by José Ferreira Thedim, *Our Lady of Fátima* (1920).
Public domain image via Wikimedia Commons.
Source: https://commons.wikimedia.org/wiki/File:First_Sculpture_of_Our_Lady_of_Fatima.jpg

St. Peter's Basilica Interior —
Public domain photograph of the interior of St. Peter's Basilica.
Public domain image via Wikimedia Commons.
Source: https://commons.wikimedia.org/wiki/File:Altar_of_St_Peter%27s_Basilica.jpg

Engraving of Pope John XII —
Public domain engraving from *The Lives and Times of the Popes* (1842) by Chevalier Artaud de Montor.
Public domain image via Wikimedia Commons.
Source: https://commons.wikimedia.org/wiki/File:Pope_John_XII.jpg

Engraving of Marozia of Tusculum —
Public domain engraving, c. 1842. Frequently reproduced in historical works, including *The Lives and Times of the Popes* and related biographical collections.
Source: https://en.wikipedia.org/wiki/Marozia#/media/File:Marozia.jpg

Reliquary of Saint Munditia —
Photograph of the relic of Saint Munditia, a 4th-century martyr, housed in St. Peter's Church, Munich, Germany. Public

domain image widely reproduced in religious art and relic discussions. Wikipedia.

Source: https://en.wikipedia.org/wiki/Munditia#/media/File: 2022-04-26_St._Peter_Munich_Interior_26.jpg

Witches Presenting Wax Dolls to the Devil — 18th-century woodcut illustrating witchcraft and ritual sacrifice. Public domain.

Source: The Public Domain Review.

https://pdimagearchive.org/images/3e40fe19-e65a-4f8b-b02b-3d16a427ea76/

Cathedral Interior —

The Cathedral Basilica of Saints Peter and Paul symbolizes ritualism without substance.

Public domain image via Wikimedia Commons.

Source: https://commons.wikimedia.org/wiki/File:Interior_of_the_Cathedral_Basilica_of_Saints_Peter_and_Paul.JPG

House Church in China —

Photo of underground Christian worshippers in China gathered in a small home setting. Reflects early church simplicity and faith under pressure.

ChinaAid via Wikimedia Commons. Licensed under CC BY-SA 4.0.

Source: https://en.wikipedia.org/wiki/House_church_%28China%29

St. Peter's Basilica at Dusk —

View of Ponte Sant'Angelo and St. Peter's Basilica in the distance. Symbolizes Rome's spiritual dominance and its shift from early Christian faith to ritualized power.

Ben Mitchell, *St. Peter's Basilica at Dusk* (July 6, 2006), via Wikimedia Commons. Licensed under CC BY-SA 2.5.

Source: https://commons.wikimedia.org/wiki/File:Sant%27Angelo_bridge,_dusk,_Rome,_Italy.jpg

Vatican Apostolic Archives —
Interior image of the Vatican's restricted archives, illustrating institutional secrecy and information control.
Public domain via Wikimedia Commons.
Source: https://commons.wikimedia.org/wiki/File:Interiors_of_Vatican_Secret_Archives.png

Medieval Manuscript: Codex Vaticanus B —
Image of a manuscript page from the Vatican's 4th-century Greek Bible, emphasizing preservation vs. accessibility.
Public domain via Wikipedia.
Source: https://en.wikipedia.org/wiki/Codex_Vaticanus

Hidden Archives — A photograph of a gloved archivist handling an ancient manuscript, symbolizing the secretive preservation of religious texts.
Source: Image: Stockcake (AI-generated), free for commercial use.

Hands in Chains — Spiritual Freedom —
Artistic image showing broken chains and raised fists, symbolizing deliverance from oppression and false systems.
Source: Public domain image, PublicDomainPictures.net

St. Catherine's Greek Manuscript — John 13:1–9 —
An ancient Greek lectionary fragment preserved in Mt. Sinai's

historic monastery, pointing to the purity of Christ's words outside Vatican control.

Source: Public domain manuscript from St. Catherine's Monastery. Sourced via the Library of Congress and *The Text of the Gospels* blog.

Open Church Door: Departure Toward Christ —

Symbolic photo of a shadowed cathedral interior with sunlight pouring through an open door, representing the spiritual awakening that often begins with leaving religious institutions.

Source: Public domain image, PublicDomainPictures.net

Silent Departure: Walking Into the Light —

A figure steps through a narrow doorway into sunlight, symbolizing the quiet courage of those leaving religious systems in search of Christ's truth.

Licensed for commercial use (royalty-free).

Source: StockCake, https://stockcake.com/i/threshold-of-light_2677435_1518222

Tears in the Pew: A Cry of Awakening —

A woman weeps alone in a church pew, symbolizing the pain of disillusionment and the deep emotional cost of walking away from deception.

Royalty-free image licensed for commercial use via Pexels.

Source: https://www.pexels.com/photo/woman-leaning-on-a-bench-6284260/

TERMS
BIBLICAL CONTRAST

Mass

Latin *missa*, related to dismissal or sacrifice; tied to Roman Catholic Eucharistic sacrifice

The Lord's Supper is a remembrance, not a repeated sacrifice (Luke 22:19; Hebrews 10:10-14)

Easter

Derived from *Eostre*, a Germanic fertility goddess

Passover (Pesach) is the biblical commemoration (Exodus 12; Luke 22:15)

Sacrament

Latin *sacramentum*, used in Roman military oaths

The Bible refers to baptism and the Lord's Supper as acts of obedience, not mystical rites (Romans 6:3-4; 1 Corinthians 11:24-26)

Lent

From Anglo-Saxon *lencten* (spring); rooted in pre-Christian fasting rituals

New Testament fasting is voluntary and Spirit-led (Matthew 6:16-18)

Priest (New Covenant context)

Derived from the Old Covenant temple system and pagan mediator roles All believers are priests (I Peter 2:9); Jesus is our High Priest (Hebrews 4:14-16)

Holy Father

Pagan Rome used similar titles for emperors; also used for Jupiter

Jesus said to call no man "father" in a spiritual sense (Matthew 23:9)

Cathedral

From Latin *cathedra* (seat of authority), linked to imperial rule

The early Church met in homes and had no central governing seats (Acts 2:46; Romans 16:5)

Confirmation

Modeled after Roman coming-of-age rites

The Holy Spirit is received at new birth, not by institutional ceremony (Acts 2:38; Galatians 3:2)

Advent

Latin *adventus*, meaning "arrival," is based on ancient imperial celebrations

The Bible calls believers to await Christ's return, not reenact seasonal liturgy (Titus 2:13)

Clergy / Laity

Greek *kleros* (lot) vs. *laos* (people); developed into a hierarchy

The New Testament shows a shared priesthood and mutual service (1 Peter 2:5; Ephesians 4:11-13)

Why This Matters

Language shapes belief. If we casually adopt words and concepts without understanding their origins, we risk:

- Repeating empty rituals
- Inheriting deception
- Calling holy what God never ordained

The gospel isn't built on pagan terms. It's built on a crucified and risen Savior.

> *"You nullify the word of God by your tradition that you have handed down. And you do many other similar things." (Mark 7:13).*

> *"Test everything; hold fast to what is good." (1 Thessalonians 5:21).*

Let your words reflect your worship. And let your worship reflect the Word.

PART VI

TOOLS FOR THE EXIT

PRACTICAL READER ADD-ONS

READER DISCUSSION GUIDE
INDIVIDUAL OR GROUP USE

1. Which traditions or teachings in your church experience have you accepted without question?

2. How has learning about the "Constantine shift" altered your understanding of Christianity's development?

3. What does *spiritual transformation* mean to you personally, beyond belief or behavior?

4. In what areas of your life do you still feel shaped more by religion than by a direct relationship with Jesus?

5. Which chapter or appendix impacted you most, and why?

6. What truth in this book challenged you the most—or made you uncomfortable—and how did you respond?

7. Have you spent time in prayer reflecting on the themes in this book? If not, what hesitations or questions remain?

8. What steps, if any, do you feel led to take in response to what you've read?

9. How can followers of Christ pursue truth without judgment, pride, or division?

10. How can the Body of Christ move forward with greater humility, unity, and spiritual integrity?

11. What do you sense God calling you to do with what you have now examined and understood?

RECOMMENDED RESOURCES
DEEP DIVE LINKS

These sources offer deeper study on themes explored in this book. While not all agree with one another doctrinally, each brings valuable insight. Always use biblical discernment and compare everything to the Word of God.

I. Key Authors Referenced

Ed Kurath

- *I Will Give You Rest*. Post Falls, ID: Divinely Designed, 2003.
- *Transformation New Testament and Commentary*. Golden, CO: Self-published, 2023.
- *You Can Read the Greek: The Easy Way,* Golden, CO: Divinely Designed, 2015.

About Ed Kurath

Ed Kurath is a Christian prayer minister, Bible teacher, and author known for his deep focus on healing, spiritual transformation, and the literal meaning of the New Testament. He holds a master's degree in counseling from Denver Seminary and completed an internship and residency at Elijah House Ministries, where he also served as a staff counselor for four years.

For nearly two decades, Ed was a Licensed Professional Counselor and Marriage and Family Therapist in Idaho before fully transitioning into Christ-centered ministry. Today, he ministers in the Denver, Colorado area, helping individuals and couples experience heart-level healing through the transforming power of Jesus Christ.

After a personal crisis in 1985, Ed experienced profound healing through the Lord's direct intervention. That transformation reshaped his life and calling. He now devotes himself to sharing the message of true spiritual freedom, emphasizing that healing is not just possible —it is promised through Christ.

Learn more at: www.divinelydesigned.com/abouted

Tom Horn & Cris Putnam

- *Exo-Vaticana: Petrus Romanus, Project L.U.C.I.F.E.R., and the Vatican's Astonishing Plan for the Arrival of an Alien Savior*. Crane, MO: Defender Publishing, 2013.

Avro Manhattan

- *The Vatican's Holocaust*. Chino, CA: Chick Publications, 1986.

Alexander Hislop

- *The Two Babylons*. London: S.W. Partridge & Co., 1853.

Dave Hunt

- *A Woman Rides the Beast*. Eugene, OR: Harvest House, 1994.

Watchman Nee

- *The Normal Christian Life*. Wheaton, IL: Tyndale House, 1957.

A.W. Tozer

- *The Knowledge of the Holy*. San Francisco: Harper & Row, 1961.

Leonard Ravenhill

- *Why Revival Tarries*. Minneapolis, MN: Bethany Fellowship, 1959.

II. Online Study Tools & Historical Research Platforms

These sites offer access to church history, Greek tools, and translation comparisons.

- **Bible Gateway.com** — Online Bible study tool offering dozens of translations, keyword search, and parallel verse comparison.
- **Blue Letter Bible.org** — Greek/Hebrew tools, interlinear study, Strong's concordance integration.

- **Christian History Institute.org** — Concise history of church councils, reformers, martyrs.

III. Prophetic & Investigative Research

(*Use discernment when exploring prophetic claims or speculative history.*)

- **ChristianityBeliefs.org** — Bible prophecy studies and critiques of Catholic doctrine from a pre-millennial historicist lens.
- **ChristianObserver.net** — Historicist interpretations of
- end-times prophecy and Vatican involvement in global agendas.
- **AmazingDiscoveries.org** — Jesuit and prophecy exposés from a Seventh-day Adventist worldview, featuring the "Total Onslaught" series.
- **ProphesyAgain.org** — Sermons and videos on Revelation, Catholic ecumenism, and the final test facing God's remnant people.

IV. Alternative Viewpoints

(*Use with Discernment*)

- **End Time Delusions** (Steve Wohlberg) — Challenges dispensationalism and futurist rapture theology from a historicist, Adventist-influenced Protestant view.
- **The Farsight Institute** (Farsight.org) — Remote viewing research organization investigating global phenomena, alien agendas, ancient civilizations, and religious institutions.

- *Exo-Vaticana*: *Petrus Romanus, Project L.U.C.I.F.E.R. and the Vatican's Astonishing Plan for the Arrival of an Alien Savior* (Horn & Putnam) — Explores the Vatican's involvement in extraterrestrial disclosure using a mix of theology, government source analysis, and speculative evidence.

*Inclusion of a source does not imply endorsement of every doctrine. Test all spirits, hold fast what is true (1 Thessalonians 5:21).

TRILOGY PREVIEW

Book Two — *The False Christ of Rome: Rome's Last Crusade Against the True Jesus*

> *"She has become a dwelling place for demons... For all the nations have drunk the wine of her immorality."*
> *(Revelation 18:2–3)*

**Book One exposed the origin of Rome's deception.
Book Two reveals how that deception is being operationalized.**

The False Christ of Rome examines how the modern Vatican is positioning itself for a unified global spiritual system through ecumenism, technotheology, and the strategic rebranding of ancient authority in modern language.

This volume follows the evidence behind:

- The Vatican's push toward global religious convergence

- The role of Jesuit influence in education, law, and theology
- The revival of cosmic and "non-human" narratives within Catholic teaching
- The merging of religion, technology, and authority into a single moral framework

What once relied on ritual and empire is now being reinforced through systems that appear humanitarian, inclusive, and enlightened—yet quietly centralize spiritual authority.

The deception is no longer confined to Rome.
It is global, adaptive, and increasingly digital.

Additional resources, order links, and early access materials are available at:
www.brianmalek.com
The False Christ of Rome is **now available** and continues the investigation into Rome's modern spiritual infrastructure.

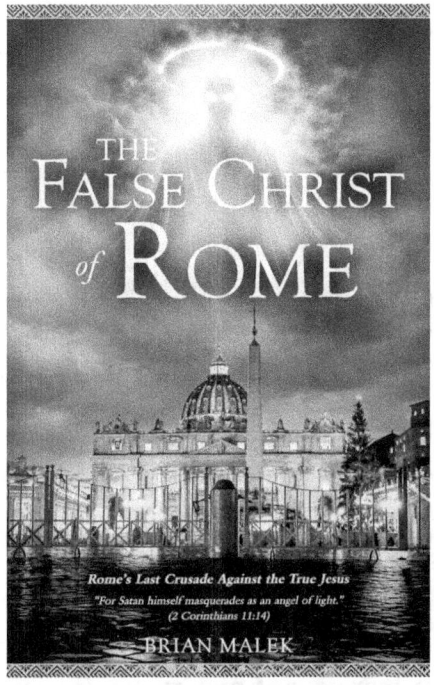

The False Christ of Rome: Rome's Last Crusade Against the True Jesus

Book Three — *The Gospel Recovered: The Bible They Tried to Bury* (Coming Soon)

Before Rome constructed a global religious system, it reshaped something more foundational: the language of the faith itself. Because the New Testament is not merely devotional literature—it is carefully structured revelation. And when structure is altered, systems follow.

The Gospel Recovered returns to the original Koine Greek of the New Testament to examine how translation decisions, theological framing, and institutional influence gradually altered how generations understood repentance, grace, sanctification, and life in Christ.

This final installment of the trilogy moves from exposure to recovery.

Inside, you'll explore:

- The original Greek meaning of key words that define salvation and transformation
- How certain translation traditions shifted emphasis from inner renewal to external compliance
- Why repentance (metanoia) was recast as ritual rather than radical change of mind
- How sanctification was reframed as moral performance instead of Spirit-formed life
- What the apostles actually proclaimed about identity, freedom, and participation in Christ

Drawing from manuscript history, linguistic analysis, and the work of scholars who prioritized textual fidelity, this book does not argue for novelty. It argues for clarity.

This is not an attack on Scripture.

It is a defense of it.

Not a rejection of faith, but a return to its source.

Because when the language is restored, the message becomes clear again.

And when the message is clear, transformation follows — not through institution, but through the indwelling life of Christ Himself.

ABOUT THE AUTHOR

Brian Malek is a nonfiction investigative author focused on exposing spiritual deception within institutional Christianity. Raised in a devout Roman Catholic household—his mother a parish secretary and his father a Fourth Degree Knight of Columbus—he developed an early familiarity with Catholic doctrine, hierarchy, and ritual that later shaped his research.

By profession, Malek is a commercial airline pilot. Outside the cockpit, his work centers on historical theology, suppressed church history, and the divergence between New Testament Christianity and religious systems of control. His writing emphasizes documented sources, Scripture, and historical continuity rather than denominational polemics.

His debut book, *The Devil in the Holy City*, is a carefully researched exposé examining the pagan, imperial, and doctrinal foundations of the Roman Catholic system and its lasting influence on modern Christianity.

When not researching or writing, he can usually be found mountain biking or hiking Colorado's trails with his wife and their two Jack Russell Terriers. Additional research materials and updates are available at **www.brianmalek.com.**

Author Brian Malek

BIBLIOGRAPHY

Bagatti, Bellarmino. "Recent Discoveries in the Field of Christian Archaeology." *Studium Biblicum Franciscanum Liber Annuus* 22 (1972): 5–38. Jerusalem: Franciscan Printing Press.

Bainton, Roland H. *Here I Stand: A Life of Martin Luther*. Nashville: Abingdon Press, 1950.

Barna Group. *The State of Pastors*. Ventura, CA: Barna Group, 2017.

Bercot, D. W. *Will the Real Heretics Please Stand Up*. Amberson, PA: Scroll Publishing, 1999.

———— *A Dictionary of Early Christian Beliefs*. Peabody, MA: Hendrickson Publishers, 1998.

Berry, Jason, and Gerald Renner. *Vows of Silence: The Abuse of Power in the Papacy of John Paul II*. New York: Free Press, 2004.

Brown, Michael. *Apostolic Succession and the Papacy: The Vatican's Claims in Light of Scripture and*
History. TruthWatch Publishing, 2016.

Brown, Raymond E. *Peter in the New Testament*. Augsburg Fortress, 1973.

Catechism of the Catholic Church. 2nd ed. Vatican City: Libreria Editrice Vaticana, 1997.

Le Catholique National. Bern, Switzerland. July 13, 1895.

"Christians Decide to Put Aside Their Petty Differences and Unite for the Gospel— Haha Just Kidding, We're Fighting Each Other Online." *The Babylon Bee*. June 14, 2024. https://babylonbee.com/news/christians-decide-to-put-aside-their-petty-differences-and-unite-for-the-gospel-haha-just-kidding-were-fighting-each-other-online.

Ciappi, Mario Luigi. Personal correspondence and theological summaries.

Ciarrocchi, Joseph W. *The Doubting Disease: Help for Scrupulosity and Religious Compulsions*. Mahwah, NJ: Paulist Press, 1995.

Clermont-Ganneau, Charles. "Jewish-Christian Tombs on the Mount of Olives." *Palestine Exploration Fund Quarterly Statement* 5 (1873): 122–132. London: Palestine Exploration Fund.

Congregation for the Doctrine of the Faith. *The Message of Fatima*. Vatican City: Libreria Editrice Vaticana, 2000. https://www.vatican.va.

Cornwell, John. *Hitler's Pope: The Secret History of Pius XII*. New York: Viking, 1999.

Danker, Frederick William, ed. *A Greek-English Lexicon of the New Testament and Other Early Christian Literature*. 3rd ed. Chicago: University of Chicago Press, 2000.

Drake, H. A. *Constantine and the Bishops: The Politics of Intolerance*. Baltimore: Johns Hopkins University Press, 2000.

"Document on Human Fraternity." https://www.vatican.va. 2019.

Eusebius. *Ecclesiastical History*. Translated by C. F. Cruse. Grand Rapids, MI: Baker Book House, 1955.

———. *Life of Constantine*. Translated by Averil Cameron and Stuart G. Hall. Oxford: Clarendon Press, 1999.

Ferrua, Antonio. As cited in *The Devil in the Holy City: Original Master Manuscript* (private archival correspondence, 2025).

Fox, George. *The Journal of George Fox*. Edited by Norman Penney. Cambridge: Cambridge University Press, 1911.

Fuller Institute. "Pastoral Ministry Survey." 1991.

Gilson, Étienne. *The Christian Philosophy of St. Thomas Aquinas*. New York: Random House, 1956.

Guarducci, Margherita. *The Tomb of St. Peter*. New York: Hawthorn Books, 1960.

Hislop, Alexander. *The Two Babylons*. 2nd ed. Ontario, CA: Chick Publications, 1998.

Horn, Thomas, and Cris Putnam. *Exo-Vaticana: Petrus Romanus, Project L.U.C.I.F.E.R., and the Vatican's Astonishing Plan for the Arrival of an Alien Savior*. Crane, MO: Defender Publishing, 2013.

Hunt, Dave. *A Woman Rides the Beast: The Roman Catholic Church and the Last Days*. Eugene, OR: Harvest House Publishers, 1994.

———. *What Love Is This? Calvinism's Misrepresentation of God*. Bend, OR: The Berean Call, 2002.

Jerome. *Commentary on Matthew*. In *Patrologia Latina*, vol. 26. Edited by J.-P. Migne. Paris, 1844–1864.

———. *De Viris Illustribus*. Translated by Thomas P. Halton. Washington, DC: Catholic University of America Press, 1999.

Kurath, Edward. *I Will Give You Rest*. Post Falls, ID: Divinely Designed, 2003.

———. *Transformation in the Epistles*. Revised ed. Post Falls, ID: Divinely Designed, 2019.

———.*Transformation New Testament and Commentary*, Rev. 14 First Printing (Golden, CO: Divinely Designed, 2022).

———. *You Can Read the Greek: The Easy Way*, (Golden, CO: Divinely Designed, 2015).

———. *Key Verses*. Unpublished manuscript, n.d.

Lifeway Research. "Pastors' Mental Health and Burnout." 2021. https://lifewayresearch.com.

Luther, Martin. *Smalcald Articles*. 1537.

Lutheran–Roman Catholic Commission on Unity. *From Conflict to Communion*. 2013. https://www.vatican.va.

MacMullen, Ramsay. *Christianity and Paganism in the Fourth to Eighth Centuries*. New Haven: Yale University Press, 1997.

Manhattan, Avro. *The Vatican Billions*. Chino, CA: Chick Publications, 1983.

————. *The Vatican's Holocaust*. Chino, CA: Chick Publications, 1986.

Marshall, Taylor. *Infiltration: The Plot to Destroy the Church from Within*. Manchester, NH: Sophia Institute Press, 2019.

Martin, Malachi. *The Keys of This Blood*. New York: Simon & Schuster, 1990.

Nee, Watchman. *The Normal Christian Life*. Wheaton, IL: Tyndale House, 1977.

Paris, Edmond. *The Secret History of the Jesuits*. Chino, CA: Chick Publications, 1975.

Pew Research Center. "In U.S., Decline of Christianity Continues at Rapid Pace." October 17, 2019. https://www.pewresearch.org.

Phelps, Eric Jon. *Vatican Assassins*. 3rd ed. Lowvehm Publishing, 2007.

Pope Leo X. *Exsurge Domine*. June 15, 1520.

Pope Leo XIII. *Humanum Genus*. April 20, 1884. https://www.vatican.va.

————. *Praeclara Gratulationis Publicae (On the Reunion of Christendom)*. Encyclical letter, June 20, 1894.

Pope Paul VI. Homily for the Solemnity of Saints Peter and Paul. June 29, 1972. https://www.vatican.va.

————. "General Audience." June 26, 1968.

Pope Pius XII. "Radio Message Announcing the Discovery of the Tomb of St. Peter." December 23, 1950.

Rainer, Thom. "Why Pastors Leave Ministry." 2019.

Ravenhill, Leonard. *Why Revival Tarries*. Minneapolis, MN: Bethany Fellowship, 1959.

De Rosa, Peter. *Vicars of Christ: The Dark Side of the Papacy.* New York: Crown Publishing Group, 1988.

Sadler, I. A. *Mystery Babylon the Great: The Church of Rome and the European Union Exposed to the Light of Truth.* Reading, UK: I. A. Sadler, 2002.

Schaff, Philip. *History of the Christian Church.* Vol. 3. Grand Rapids, MI: Eerdmans, 1910.

Second Vatican Council. *Nostra Aetate.* October 28, 1965.

Strong, James. *The Exhaustive Concordance of the Bible.* Nashville: Abingdon, 1890.

Sunshine, Glenn. *Why You Think the Way You Do.* Grand Rapids, MI: Zondervan, 2009.

The Alta Vendita. *Permanent Instruction of the Alta Vendita,* Nineteenth century. Reproduced in various editions; cited in Taylor Marshall, *Infiltration: The Plot to Destroy the Church from Within.* Manchester, NH: Sophia Institute Press, 2019.

Tozer, A.W. *The Pursuit of God.* Harrisburg, PA: Christian Publications, 1948.

————. *The Knowledge of the Holy.* New York: Harper & Row, 1961.

Viganò, Carlo Maria. "Open Letter to President Donald Trump." October 25, 2020.

Viola, Frank, and George Barna. *Pagan Christianity?* Carol Stream, IL: Tyndale House Publishers, 2008.

Vatican. "Document on Human Fraternity for World Peace and Living Together." February 4, 2019. https://www.vatican.va.

Vatican Apostolic Archive. "Rescript of the Holy Father Francis." October 28, 2019. https://www.vatican.va.

Veith, Walter. *Truth Matters.* Ontario, Canada: Amazing Discoveries, 2002.

Walsh, John Evangelist. *The Bones of Saint Peter.* New York: Image Books, 1985.

Webster, William. *The Church of Rome at the Bar of History*. Edinburgh: Banner of Truth Trust, 1995.

Woodrow, Ralph. *Babylon Mystery Religion*. Riverside, CA: Woodrow Evangelistic Association, 1966.

THEME INDEX

False Religion

- Chapter 3
- Chapter 4
- Chapter 5
- Chapter 7
- Chapter 8
- Chapter 9
- Chapter 10
- Chapter 11
- Chapter 12
- Chapter 13
- Chapter 14
- Chapter 15
- Chapter 16

Freedom from Bondage

- Appendix A
- Appendix B
- Appendix C
- Appendix D
- Appendix E
- Appendix F
- Appendix I
- Appendix J
- Appendix L
- Appendix M
- Appendix P
- Bonus Chapter: *Voices from the Exit Door*
- Chapter 1
- Chapter 2
- Chapter 3
- Chapter 4

Catholic Doctrines Exposed

Spiritual Warfare

Biblical Truth Restored

Religious Spirits

BACK COVER

"Never has something so black and wicked gotten away with appearing so holy and mysteriously beautiful... for so long." ~ Keith Green

For centuries, the Roman Catholic Church has shaped Western civilization under the claim of divine authority. But beneath its cathedrals, rituals, and traditions lies a system built on political power, pagan influence, and doctrinal distortion.

The Devil in the Holy City is a meticulously researched exposé revealing how Rome merged Christianity with ancient paganism, replaced spiritual transformation with religious control, and constructed a counterfeit gospel that spread far beyond Catholicism itself—an illusion of holiness that has endured for centuries.

Inside this book, you'll uncover:

- The hidden history, documented corruption, and systemic failures of the Roman Catholic institution

- How Catholic doctrine absorbed pagan rituals and imperial theology
- Biblical warnings about false religion and spiritual deception
- Why this system continues to influence modern Christianity
- How to break the spiritual bondage imposed by Rome's false gospel

This is not an attack on individual believers—but an examination of an institution that claims Christ's authority while contradicting His teachings.

Written by a former Catholic who followed the evidence wherever it led, *The Devil in the Holy City* calls readers to discernment, freedom, and truth.

The question is no longer whether deception exists—but whether you will examine it for yourself.

www.ingramcontent.com/pod-product-compliance
Lightning Source LLC
Chambersburg PA
CBHW070546130626
46556CB00001B/41